Eight True Stories About Women

Who Made a Difference

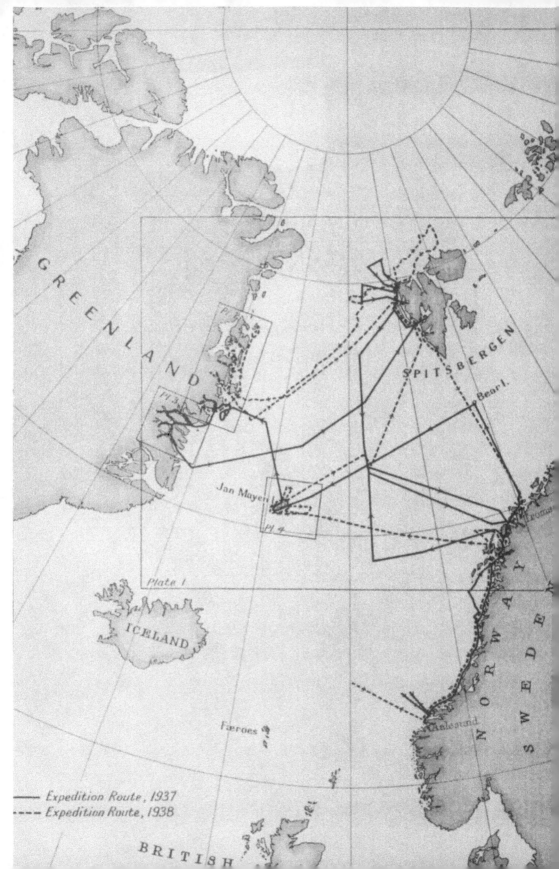

GREENLAND

SPITSBERGEN

Bear I.

Jan Mayen

Pl. 4

Plate 1

ICELAND

NORWAY

SWEDEN

Tromsø

Ålesund

Færoes

Expedition Route, 1937
Expedition Route, 1938

BRITISH

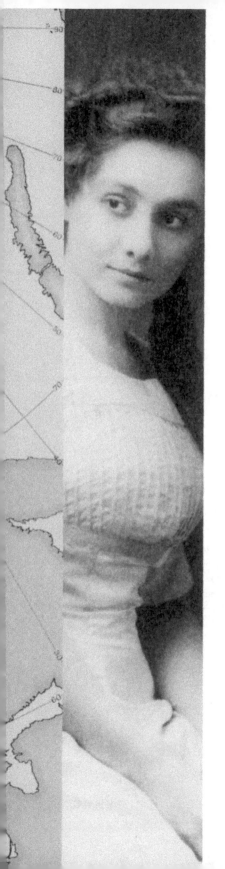

W✦MEN

Eight True Stories About
Women Who Made a Difference

PENNY COLMAN

HENRY HOLT AND COMPANY • NEW YORK

To Sophie Colman de Haën:
This book is for you with my love forever.

Henry Holt and Company, LLC
Publishers since 1866
175 Fifth Avenue
New York, New York 10010
www.henryholtchildrensbooks.com

Henry Holt® is a registered trademark of Henry Holt and Company, LLC.

Library of Congress Cataloging-in-Publication Data
Colman, Penny.
Adventurous women : eight true stories about women who made a difference /
Penny Colman.—1st ed.
p.   cm.
Includes bibliographical references.
Contents: Cold? yes . . . I love it, Louise Arner Boyd: Arctic explorer—Blank spots
on the maps, Mary Gibson Henry: plant hunter—A preeminent woman, Juana
Briones: enterprising family head—Great clouds of yellow and orange fumes, Alice
Hamilton: supersleuth—I will build them again, Mary McLeod Bethune:
passionate educator—Whirlwind of work, Katharine Wormeley: daring
superintendent; letter excerpts—For the sum of love and affection and ten dollars,
Biddy Mason: fierce fighter—To be somebody, Peggy Hull: resolute reporter.
ISBN 978-0-8050-9737-5
1. Adventure and adventurers—Biography.   2. Women adventurers—Biography.
3. Women—Biography. I. Title.

CT9970.C65 2006   920.72—dc22 [B]   2005050311

First Edition—2006
Printed in the United States of America on acid-free paper. ∞

P1

CONTENTS

ADVENTUROUS WOMEN

Eight True Stories About Women

Who Made a Difference

Author's Note

MY GREAT-UNCLE Walter Granger was a famous fossil collector and vertebrate paleontologist. He was born in 1872 and died in 1941. I was born in 1944, and my parents named me Penelope Granger Morgan.

All my life, I heard stories about Uncle Walter and his wife, Anna, known as "Annie." How he searched for dinosaurs and extinct mammals and fossil primates throughout the American West and Egypt and China and Mongolia. How he and his assistants discovered the first whole dinosaur eggs and nest. How Annie worked with Walter in China for almost ten years and published several articles in *Natural History*, including one titled "Rescuing a Little-known Chinese Art: How an Explorer's Wife 'Discovered' a Fascinating Style of Peasant Embroidery in Far Western China, and Helped to Save It from Oblivion."

Walter and Annie Granger were not the only adventurers in

my family. There was my mother, who compiled a lifetime of adventures in everything from travel to journalism to art to music to firefighting. Yes, firefighting; as I write this I am glancing at a photograph of my mother taken shortly after she helped put out a big fire. She is wearily leaning against a pole and holding her helmet in one hand and a cup of something to drink in the other.

My mother was fifty years old when she joined the Chautauqua Volunteer Fire Company—actually, she was a few months short of her fiftieth birthday. I remember that because she had to pass the tests before she reached fifty, the age limit for new members.

No wonder I grew up loving adventures and believing that women could have adventures, even though women were rarely, if ever, portrayed as adventurers in books or in the movies or on television.

For me, adventures are about being bold, about defying set ways of thinking and behaving, about taking risks, going beyond the boundaries, the limitations, about overcoming obstacles, about daring to be different. Adventures can happen anywhere—in a laboratory or a library, at home or far away. Adventures do not discriminate: Anyone can have one—women, children, men of any age or race, ethnicity, ability, sexual orientation, religion. I selected women because most adventure stories are about men, especially historical adventure stories. My intent is not to replace men but to add women.

Adventurous Women features eight women from diverse racial and ethnic backgrounds: Louise Boyd, an Arctic explorer; Mary Gibson Henry, a botanist and plant hunter; Juana Briones, an entrepreneur and family head; Alice Hamilton, a scientist and industrial toxicologist; Mary McLeod Bethune, an educator and humanitarian; Katharine Wormeley, a Civil War superintendent on hospital transport ships; Biddy Mason, a former slave, midwife, landowner, and church founder; and Peggy Hull, a journalist and war correspondent. They were all born in the 1800s and died in the 1900s, except Juana Briones who died in 1889 and Biddy Mason who died in 1891. Two of the women—Boyd and Briones—grew up on the West Coast of the United States. Henry and Wormeley grew up on the East Coast. Hamilton and Hull grew up in the Midwest. Mason and Bethune grew up in the South.

Four of the women—Henry, Briones, Bethune, and Hull— had husbands (Hull had several, and Briones and Bethune eventually lived apart from their husbands). Briones had eleven children, Henry had five, Mason had three, and Bethune had one. Juana Briones and Biddy Mason had no formal education. Louise Boyd, Mary Gibson Henry, and Katharine Wormeley went to finishing schools. Mary McLeod Bethune graduated from college. Alice Hamilton studied at home and at a finishing school. After that, she graduated from medical school and continued her studies at universities in Europe and in the United States.

All of the women dealt with limitations and stereotypes because they were women. They all took risks and overcame obstacles. Although a few women had access to family money, most of them generated the resources they needed through gainful employment, fund-raising, and business enterprises.

For each of the women I chose to write about, there were many more I set aside for another writing day. How did I choose? I was looking for variety and unknown women as well as known. I was looking for obvious adventures (exploring the Arctic) and not so obvious (starting a school) and for adventures that contributed something to society, that made a difference.

My research involved doing what journalists call "shoe leather research," or going places, talking to people, and searching far and wide for facts and details and true stories. I visited places that were important in the women's lives, such as Moosehead Lake in Maine where Mary Gibson Henry first fell in love with a flower and Los Angeles, California, where Biddy Mason was a midwife. I searched for information in historical societies, libraries, archives, cemeteries, public monuments, historic sites, and on the Internet. One beautiful fall day in New York City, I took my eleven-month-old granddaughter on her first library research trip to the Health Sciences Library of Columbia University where I located Alice Hamilton's original reports on lead poisoning.

I also spent innumerable hours reading. I read rolls of microfilm that contained photographic reproductions of old newspaper and magazine articles. I read scientific reports, books, letters, and speeches. I studied numerous photographs and maps. I also consulted with other historians, in particular Jeanne Farr McDonnell, an expert on Juana Briones, who provided invaluable information. Two of Mary Henry Gibson's granddaughters, Susan Pepper Treadway, president and director, Henry Foundation for Botanical Research, and Betsey Warren Davis, curator of the Mary Henry Gibson Archives, shared their knowledge about their grandmother with me. "I shall never forget the many good times after the day's work was done," Davis recalled. "At the dinner table and around the fire, all in her company enjoyed her hilarious sense of humor and her gifts for telling her adventure stories."

I wrote each chapter as an essay about a particular woman and her adventure, *not* a comprehensive biography. I made this decision because the essay form allowed me the freedom and flexibility to write about women who had very different adventures and who left behind varying amounts of primary source material. The chapters vary in length and structure: Some chapters feature extensive first-person and eyewitness accounts, and chapter six has two parts—an essay and letter excerpts. I become a visible author in chapter seven when I write about how I first "met" Biddy Mason. Throughout, however, I maintain a conversational voice. In addition, readers will discover quotations that are in italics and centered in the text. These are "teasers" to pique readers' curiosity.

The essays appear in the order in which I wrote them, a reflection of many things, including the availability of sources and the twists and turns of my curiosity. Readers, of course, can read them in any order. The back matter includes brief chronologies, a list of places to visit, namesakes, notes, and a bibliography and webliography.

Every book I research and write is an education. This book took me to new places, such as the fiord region of East Greenland (Louise Boyd); and taught me new terms, such as "phossy jaw" (Alice Hamilton); and introduced me to things I will never do (I hope), such as "toppling round at night in little boats, and clambering up ships' sides on little ladders" (Katharine Wormeley); and to things I would love to do, such as see "hillsides where thousands upon thousands of roses were abloom in such quantities they made the landscape quite pink" (Mary Gibson Henry).

Every book is also an inspiration, especially this book, for it is about real women who did real things and in the process created real stories about the many ways there are to live a passionate and productive and adventurous life.

CHAPTER ONE

"Cold? Yes . . . I Love It"

LOUISE BOYD: ARCTIC EXPLORER

1887–1972

Louise Boyd, 1928.

LOUISE BOYD grew up in California, a green and sunny land, yet fell in love with the Arctic, a cold, very cold, region mostly covered in ice, where during the long winter months the sun never shines.

She got her "first taste of the far north" as a tourist in 1924. Four years earlier she had inherited three million dollars when her father died just a year after her mother's death. Both her brothers had died of rheumatic fever as teenagers.

Boyd had been traveling here and there trying to figure out what to do with her life. Finally, she traveled on a Norwegian steamer to Spitsbergen, an Arctic island northwest of

Greenland, and to the edge of the pack ice, a jumble of massive hunks and blocks and piles of ice that forms in the polar basin and gets carried southward by the ocean currents. Ice that for much of the year forms barriers around the thousands of islands in the Arctic region. Ice that can crush a ship that stays too long as winter is setting in.

Boyd got just a glimpse of the pack ice, but it was enough to make her determined to return to "see more of the ice," *and* to see the land that lay beyond the ice. That land was Franz Josef Land, an archipelago of about eighty-five mostly ice-covered islands in the Arctic Ocean. Two Austrian explorers had discovered it in the late 1880s and named it after Austrian emperor Franz Josef I.

"I Revel in the Cold"

Two years after her first trip, Boyd went to Tromsø, a port in Norway, and tried to charter the *Hobby*, a small ship used to hunt seals, to go to the pack ice and Franz Josef Land. The captain, however, refused her money because he believed in the old superstition that women were bad luck to have aboard a ship. Boyd "begged, pleaded and cajoled" until the captain relented.

The day and night before the *Hobby* arrived at the pack ice, Boyd stayed on deck, awake, for twenty-four hours. The captain and crew, she later explained, "could smell ice, and would stick their noses up and sniff it. And they expected me to. How could I know what ice smelled like? But I wanted to be there at the start, ready when the gates to the Arctic opened and let me enter. What was the loss of a night's sleep? Nothing!"

Thick fog prevented them from seeing the ice, but they could hear it crash and bang and groan and growl along with the rumble and roar of the wind and waves.

Hours passed as the captain guided the *Hobby* through the pack ice, sometimes ramming and grinding through solid ice, other times following open water, called a lead, that could be as small as a crack or tiny stream and as big as a lake. Finally, they were on the other side of the pack ice. The fog lifted and the sun shone and Louise Boyd surveyed the scene: "I had a feeling of regret that isolation combined with some danger, made such beauty inaccessible and known to so few. . . . I understood for the first time what an old seaman meant when he told me that once you had been to the Arctic and in the ice you never would forget it and always wanted to go back."

Boyd, whom a society reporter once described as "tall, blue-eyed, graceful, slender, erect, and elegant," had brought along four friends—Janet Coleman from San Francisco, the Count and Countess Rivadavia, and Francis De Gisbert, an expert on the polar region. Their purpose—at a time when there was little opposition to hunting and no protection of animals—was to hunt on Franz Josef Land. Boyd, credited as the first woman to set foot on Franz Josef Land, shot polar bears, including one at forty feet that was charging her. "I had a narrow escape," she later said. "Bears move at an incredibly fast pace once they are charging over the ice, and the great thing for a person to do is to keep cool."

During this trip, Boyd carefully collected "botanical specimens" from Cape Flora on Northbrook Island, including several species that had not yet been reported by anyone. She kept a written record of everything that she observed from "jagged peaks" and "dome-shaped glacier-covered mountains" and islands "positively alive with gulls" and "sheltered spots with an abundance of white and yellow flowers of the anemone ranunculus family" to the "moving, hummocky ice-fields."

A passionate photographer, Boyd shot twenty-one thousand feet of film and took seven hundred pictures in order to study the "sea and land ice as well as the topography and natural history of Arctic lands." Once some crewmen of the *Hobby* took her out in a small boat to get close-up pictures of polar bears. Suddenly gale-force winds whipped up the water and the fog encircled them. The force of the wind and waves broke up the pack ice, setting chunks of it floating perilously close to their rowboat. Hours passed before the fog lifted and they realized that, in their attempt to return to the ship, they had been rowing away from the *Hobby* instead of toward it.

At the end of the six-week expedition, Boyd said, "I revel in the cold. I have got the Arctic lure and will certainly go North again."

Boyd was back two years later, in 1928, on board the *Hobby*. She had intended to do more polar bear hunting, but instead she ended up hunting for some missing men—the famed Norwegian explorer Roald Amundsen and his five companions. Ironically, they had been searching for another lost explorer, who was rescued shortly after the plane with Amundsen and his crew disappeared. Amundsen's achievements—first to reach the South Pole, first to navigate the Northwest Passage, first to fly over the North Pole—made his disappearance front-page news. A massive search was undertaken. Thousands of people sent money to help pay for the search. Icebreakers and cruisers and warships from Norway, Sweden, France, Italy, and Russia crisscrossed the dangerous wind-whipped waters filled with ice floes and shrouded in dense fog. Ski patrols searched desolate islands.

"Ice Does Such Eerie Things"

Boyd offered the services of the *Hobby* and its crew to the Norwegian government at her expense. "We felt it a privilege to give up our plans and join in the search for Amundsen," she later wrote. Two pilots joined the crew and their seaplanes were lashed to the *Hobby's* lower deck. Boyd was in the middle of the action and took her turn standing watch, even in the midst of violent winds and thunderous waves. "Four of us stood watch around the clock," she recalled. "We would just stand there and look. Ice does such eerie things. There are illusions like mirages, and there were times we could clearly see tents. Then we'd lower boats and go off and investigate. But it always turned out the same—strange formations of ice, nothing more."

Amundsen and his companions were never found. The *Hobby* had searched for ten weeks and traveled "some 10,000 miles . . . along the west coast of Spitsbergen, east to Franz Josef Land, and from there northward in the pack ice . . . as well as westward into the Greenland Sea." The King of Norway presented Boyd with the Order of St. Olaf for her part in the search. The French government made her a Chevalier of the Legion of Honor. The French Navy presented to her a diamond-studded miniature of the medal inscribed with the words *Hommage, Reconnaissance de la Marine Française à Miss Boyd, 1928.* Her hometown newspaper published an article with the headline "Arctic Search Fun for Marin 'Tomboy.'" According to the article, "Folks here think of her as the little tomboy schoolgirl who rode her father's horses and frolicked with her two brothers . . . [but] . . . city residents are not surprised at her latest adventure. . . . She has spent years exploring the far places of the earth and every once in a while, comes home to say howdy and good-bye."

Her experiences on board the *Hobby* gave Boyd invaluable information about cruising in polar seas. Feeling ready to tackle even more hazardous waters, she planned to undertake an expedition in 1931 across the Greenland Sea to the east coast of Greenland, a region that was typically blocked by an ice belt as much as 150 miles wide. Her purpose was to photograph "every fiord and sound in the region of Franz Josef and King Oscar fords," part of the largest and most complex fiord region in the world. The region was a land, Boyd explained, "where deep inlets cleave the coast and run back among the mountains as far as 120 miles (190 km), . . . where walls of rock, bizarre in form and brilliant in color, rise to heights of more than a mile above the calm waters of the fiords; where mighty glaciers come down from the inland ice cap to the fiord heads and spill over the valley walls."

"Land of Extraordinary Grandeur"

Boyd chartered a bigger, sturdier vessel, the *Veleskari*, a 125-foot-long and 27-foot-wide sealing vessel made of oak and greenheart planking with a mast of California pine and a coal-burning engine; hired a seasoned captain and crew; invited R. H. Menzies, a botanist, to join her; and assembled supplies: 250 tons of coal, 1,155 tons of fuel oil for the motor dory and other small boats, 9 tons of drinking water (23 more tons were pumped on board from melting icebergs and used during the voyage), photographic and botanical equipment and surveying instruments, 9 tents and 27 sleeping bags, and enough food for the voyage plus an additional three months. Her list of clothing for the summer expedition included an oilskin coat and hip rubber boots ("needed for when the deck is rail-under in sea water"), woolen underwear, sweaters, breeches, hobnailed boots, woolen muffler, fur cap, and woolen mittens.

Weather and ice conditions for this expedition were terrible. At times, the ice towered above the ship's railing. The captain spent days in the crow's nest searching for openings in the ice. The crew exploded dynamite that they tied to the ends of poles and stuck under the ice near the ship. "The reward of crossing this belt of ice," Boyd later wrote, "is access to a land of extraordinary grandeur and beauty."

The expedition was a great success. Boyd visited every fiord and sound, made many shore trips, took thousands of photographs, collected botanical species, observed many birds and animals, visited several Inuit settlements, traveled to the inner end of the Ice Fiord, a feat no one else had yet accomplished, and she discovered a new glacier—the De Geer Glacier. All this fueled her desire to continue organizing and leading and financing scientific expeditions that would contribute to the "knowledge of that alluring region . . . its majestic scenery, its plant and animal life, its geology and physiography, and the ice."

Louise Boyd was full of confidence about her ability to organize an expedition and to deal with the demands and dangers of the Arctic region. But she had doubts about whether or not she was "suited for leadership, particularly with a group of men." Seven years later, a reporter asked her about her experiences leading men, and she replied, "As for the men, most of them go back with me each voyage. We get along fine."

In the history of Arctic exploration, Louise Boyd was the first woman to lead an expedition—undoubtedly because she had the combination of motivation and determination and ability, and, perhaps most important, the money to do it. But she was not the first woman to be an essential part of an expedition. Indigenous women had done that for years. A Chipewyan Indian woman named "Green Stocking" participated in the preparation for Sir John Franklin's harrowing overland Arctic expedition in 1819–22. Tookoolito, an Inuit from Baffin Island, was the hero among the nineteen people of the *Polaris* expedition who were stranded on the ice for six months in the late 1800s. Anarulunguaq was awarded a medal from the King of Denmark for her participation in Knud Rasmussen's 1921–24 expedition that covered twenty thousand miles.

Nevertheless, men dominated the world of Arctic exploration. Boyd eased her way through this world by not straying too far from the conventional definitions of femininity. "I like the pleasant things most women enjoy," she told a newspaper reporter, "even if I do wear breeches and boots on an expedition, even sleep in them at times. At sea, I didn't bother with my hands, except to keep them from being frozen. . . . But I powder my nose before going on deck, no matter how rough the sea is."

"Seawater Poured In"

Building on the success of her 1931 expedition, Boyd organized another one in 1933 with the help of the American Geographical Society, a professional organization that had used Boyd's extensive and detailed photographs to make large-scale topographical maps. Boyd, the leader and photographer, was joined by a surveyor, an assistant surveyor, a physiographer, a geologist, and a botanist (who developed appendicitis along the way and had to be sent back to Norway on a whaler that happened by). She added two tide gauges and a sonic depth-sounding device to the equipment.

The *Veleskari* reached open seas on July 4, and it was the third time Boyd had spent the Fourth of July in Arctic waters. Although they were in heavy seas and the ship was "railed under," Boyd reported that they celebrated by "flying Old Glory and having the best the galley could provide, while sea water poured in—to a depth of a foot on the floor of the galley—and cooking became almost an acrobatic feat."

This time the voyage across the Greenland Sea was relatively ice free, and they arrived at the east coast of Greenland in early July.

Boyd and her staff spent the next sixty days taking photographs, making maps, exploring the fiords, and studying hundreds and hundreds of icebergs of all shapes and sizes that were formed by calving, or breaking off from glaciers. She observed that icebergs were the great source of noise in the fiords:

You hear the trickle of small rivulets on the larger bergs, and the drip-drip of water splashing from their sides. The smaller ice formed from the calving of bergs makes a crackling sound in warm weather. Occasionally there is a swish against the shore of waves produced by the overturning and breaking up of some ponderous mass. Loudest of all, like the sound of cannonading, is the boom of a berg as it splits off from its parent glacier or the crash of bursting ice as a mighty berg collapses. These extraordinary sounds echo and re-echo through the fiords.

For most of August, Boyd and her party camped in the Gregory Lake and Mystery Lake valleys. "Inanimate nature seemed almost alive in these valleys," she wrote. "Changes were constantly taking place in the topography: rocks, large and small, single and in groups, constantly ripped down the steep mountainsides, forming deep troughs and rolling out on the valley floor. . . . Ice calved off from hanging glaciers thousands of feet above us and spilled its fresh white substance over the varicolored rocks."

The first week of September, the *Veleskari* had started out of Franz Josef Fiord on its homeward journey when a ferocious gale stopped them. "Nature was closing her door on us!" Boyd later wrote. "The snow of the coming winter had arrived. Extending from summit to sea level, as far as one could see, Greenland was white. . . . Nature's warning to us was: 'Go Home!'" Fortunately, after a few days, the weather improved. The *Veleskari* set sail again and, finding the Greenland Sea ice-free ("a most unusual condition," Boyd noted), reached the Lofoten Islands, Norway, in four days and two hours—record time.

Boyd planned her next two expeditions—1937 and 1938— as a unit. The American Geographical Society had recently published her book, *The Fiord Region of East Greenland*, about her earlier expeditions, and the society was eager to continue working with her. Boyd had two major objectives: to expand the use of the sonic depth-sounding device to make bottom profiles of the Greenland Sea and the fiords, and to see how far north her expedition could get.

The 1937 expedition left Alesund, Norway, on June 4 and spent two weeks cruising along the coast and stopping at off-shore islands with their rookeries, the nesting places for thousands of Arctic birds—eiders and Arctic terns and long-tailed ducks. Then they set course for Bear Island and then on to Jan Mayen Island, a desolate, volcanic island that in the seventeenth century was the site of a major whaling station. On the very rare good weather days, Mount Beerenberg was visible, and, in Boyd's words, "loomed up in majestic glory that few mountains can rival, its 8,000-foot, glacier-hung summit, a weather breeder and catcher of clouds and fog, gleaming in the sunlight." They brought mail and news to the men at the weather station and stayed several days to conduct various studies, take pictures, map a glacier, and observe the birds.

They departed, Boyd wrote, with the "all-important question . . . when and where we should meet the ice."

"A Tantalizing Game of Ice-Pack Tag"

They met the ice—dense, heavy ice and floes, some of which had fifteen-foot-high hummocks—on July 12. It took them fourteen days to bump, push, pull, wiggle, and dynamite a way through it. At times, they could see the coast of Greenland, but their progress was "a tantalizing game of ice-pack tag, a sort of hide-and-seek with the coast." Their return trip in

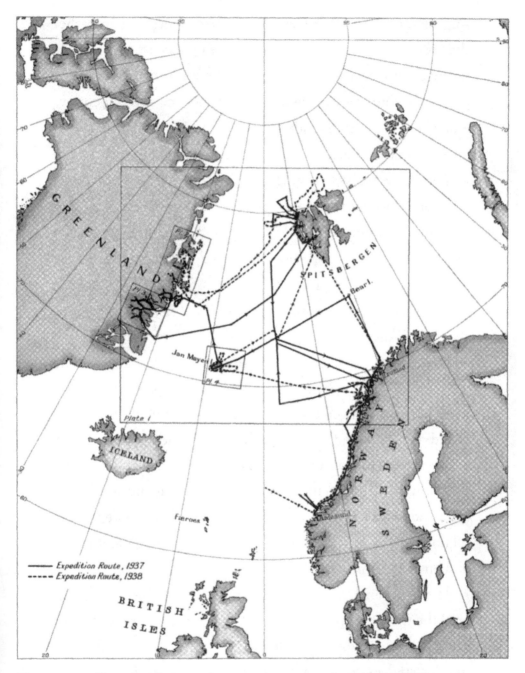

Expedition Route, 1937
Expedition Route, 1938

This route map of Louise Boyd's 1937 and 1938 expeditions appeared in her book The Coast of Northeast Greenland. *The cluster of islands on the map northeast of Spitsbergen is Franz Josef Land, the destination of Boyd's first expedition. After that adventure, she told a newspaper reporter, "I have got the Arctic lure and will certainly go North again."*

August was even more harrowing when winter set in earlier than usual and they got trapped between the coast and a belt of heavy polar ice with floes as high as the *Veleskari's* stern. At one point, the ship was "pinched" by the heavy ice and tipped several degrees over to the side. It took well-placed sticks of dynamite to get free. Faced with the prospects of being stuck for the winter or, worse yet, having the ship crushed by heavy ice, everyone on board worked day and night to find a way out. Crewmen hammered heavy ice anchors into floes to create leverage for pulling and shoving the *Veleskari* through the ice. The captain and first mate took alternating nonstop lookout shifts in the crow's nest until the ship finally broke through at the end of August.

While the ice and weather conditions in 1937 had been the worst Boyd had ever seen, they were better "than ever before" in 1938. That allowed the expedition to reach Ile de France, an island off Greenland, and make the farthest north landing ever achieved by ship on the east coast of Greenland. Along the way, Boyd and her staff of scientists visited many fiords and bays and islands where they stopped and went ashore to take pictures and gather information about the geology and plants and birds and animals.

At Bessel fiord, Boyd observed many musk oxen and gathered the wool that they had shed. "I have made a point of gathering the wool wherever I found it," she explained. She had mufflers and a sweater, dress, and jacket made for her by mem-

"When I do anything," Louise Boyd once said, "I like to do it thoroughly." She perfected her skills in photography, including photogrammetry, or taking photographs that can be used to make maps, by studying with Isaiah Bowman, a legendary photographer and director of the American Geographical Society. Her team included men who carried her heavy photographic equipment. In this picture, one man is steadying the tripod. The camera is a Fairchild Aero K 6. Boyd was the first person to use it for ground work.

bers of the Norwegian Home Industries in Alesund, Norway. According to Boyd, there was "no evidence that the Danish or Norwegian hunters or other visitors to Greenland gathered this wool; even when I told the hunters of its merit, they seemed to feel that it was not worth bothering about."

Boyd also warned "prospective photographers in East Greenland of the menace of lone musk ox bulls in certain localities." A lone musk ox bull, she reported, would attack Boyd and her crew with "a series of full-speed rushes, punctuated by halts during which he tore into the ground with horns and hoofs." A gunshot into the air usually scared the ox away. However, once they had to shoot a bull. "We got it," Boyd said, "before he got me."

The *Veleskari* arrived back in Norway in early September. The expedition had gathered a wealth of information, including the discovery of an ocean bank, or a mountain ridge, later named Louise A. Boyd Bank, along the bottom of the Greenland Sea between Bear Island and Jan Mayen Island.

The outbreak of World War II in 1939 put an end to Louise Boyd's independent expeditions. Realizing the strategic impor-tance of the region and her treasure trove of invaluable experi-ence and knowledge, Boyd volunteered her services to the United States War Department. In 1941, she led an expedition, sponsored by the U.S. government, to study the effects of polar magnetism on radio communications. In 1949, she was honored by the Department of the Army for her "outstanding patriotic service."

In 1955, Louise Boyd, at the age of sixty-eight, made her last trip to the Arctic region. This time she was in an airplane and became the first woman to fly over and around the North Pole. On board, she had the flag of the Society of Women Geogra-phers. "North, north, north we flew," she later wrote.

Soon we left all land behind us. From the cabin window I saw great stretches of ocean flecked with patches of white floating ice. . . . And as I saw the ocean change to massive fields of solid white, my heart leaped up. . . . Then—in a moment of happiness which I shall never forget—our instruments told me we were there. For directly below us, 9,000 feet down, lay the North Pole. No cloud in that brilliant blue sky hid our view of this glorious field of shining ice.

During her life, Boyd received many awards and honors, including three honorary doctorates. The Geographic Institute of Denmark named the land between the glaciers she discovered—De Geer Glacier and Jätte Glacier—Miss Boyd Land. The American Polar Society honored her. The American Geographical Society elected her to the Council of Fellows, the first woman to achieve that status in the society's 108-year history. She was elected a member of Britain's Royal Geographical Society, which had refused to admit women until 1912.

In 1967 the Explorers Club in New York City honored Boyd as "one of the world's greatest women explorers." As always, Boyd arrived elegantly dressed; this time she wore a pink dress and a spray of fresh white orchids. "I don't feel dressed unless I'm wearing flowers," she once told a reporter. "Even in Greenland, I'd find something and wear it with a safety pin." She also said that she always wore a hat. "I've never thought of going without one, unless it was to the dentist."

Louise Boyd died in sunny California in 1972. As she had requested, her cremated remains were scattered over ice-covered land.

CHAPTER TWO

"Blank Spot on the Maps"

MARY GIBSON HENRY: PLANT HUNTER

1884–1967

MARY GIBSON was seven years old and on a camping trip at Moosehead Lake in Maine when she fell in love—in love with a flower, *Linnaea borealis*, a tiny, usually pink, bell-shaped flower borne in pairs atop delicate stems that rise above a cluster of evergreen leaves. That "gem of gems," Mary later recalled, "awoke in me not only a love for and an appreciation of the absolute perfection of the flower itself, but also for the dark silent forest that shelters such treasures."

Mary came from a long line of lovers of flowers and forests, of all outdoors and things that grow. Her great-grandfather on her mother's side had the first greenhouse in Philadelphia and belonged to one of the earliest horticultural societies in North America dedicated to the science of growing fruits, vegetables, flowers, and plants. The Seckel pear was developed by and named after her great-uncle. Her grandfather on her father's side also had a greenhouse and was interested in horticulture.

But, most of all, there was her father, John Howard Gibson, who loved the outdoors.

"As a young child," Mary recalled, "I enjoyed nothing more than listening to my father tell of his hunting and camping trips, and too, to stand beside him when he was target shoot-ing. Often I was allowed a few shots. Helping to clean his rifle

Mary Gibson Henry at age fifteen.

afterward was a cherished chore. So much so that even today I like no perfume better than the aroma of a humble tube of gun grease from which nostalgia just seems to ooze."

Mary's father was the one who took her on the camping trip to Moosehead Lake where she first fell in love with *Linnaea bore-alis.* A year after that camping trip, her father died. She was eight years old. Many years later, Mary said, "His influence, that of a man who loved the outdoors and who was gentle, strong and kind, remains with me."

"We Were Roped Together"

Mary's love of the outdoors was fueled by many trips with her family. In 1902, the year she graduated from Agnes Irwin School, she traveled with an aunt in the western part of the United States. In awe of the Rocky Mountains and Grand Canyon, Mary wrote, "The magnificence of the country thrilled me beyond words." Several years later she traveled to Europe with her mother and brother. "The 'high spot' of the trip, in more ways than one," Mary wrote, "was a climb with my brother and three guides to the summit of Mont Blanc, altitude 15,781 feet. We were roped together and it was a tremendously exciting experience."

Happily and not surprisingly, Mary, a five-foot-one-inch, slight, spunky, strong-faced woman, married a man, John Norman Henry, who shared her passion for the outdoors. Their honeymoon trip included a tent and a canoe.

Mary, now known as Mary Gibson Henry, and John spent their first seventeen years together in Philadelphia, Pennsylvania. John, who was a physician, concentrated on his medical practice. Mary gave birth to five children—Mary, Josephine (also called Jo), Norman, Howard, and Frederick—and tended to their needs. They continued their love of the outdoors by going on family camping trips. Mary, however, did not have much time or space to focus on flowers and plants during these years, although she did not completely abandon her passion. They had a nice backyard, she later recalled, with "some Lilacs and Iris and Narcissus. Best of all I had a tiny greenhouse."

In 1927, the Henrys moved from Philadelphia to ninety-five acres of farmland in nearby Gladwyne, Pennsylvania. They built a new house with a greenhouse attached. But then, "great grief came to us," Mary Gibson Henry wrote, "when we lost our youngest son, aged six."

She sought solace in her passion. "I craved solitude, and working with my plants was all I cared to do," she wrote.

Henry wanted to turn their undeveloped land into an experimental garden. She wanted rare native varieties and beautiful plants and specimens she had read about in books such as *The Travels of William Bartram*, an account first published in 1791 of William Bartram's nature travels and plant hunting expeditions throughout the southeastern United States.

"Risked Life and Limb"

Plant hunting was an ancient activity. In all times and in all places, people—merchants, soldiers, missionaries, pilgrims, troubadours, healers, cooks, and travelers—collected plants and seeds and roots and carried them from one place to another. In 1482 B.C.E., Queen Hatshepsut of Egypt sent five ships to East Africa on the earliest recorded plant-hunting expedition.

Plant hunters had a variety of motives. The earliest collectors often sought plants that had medicinal values. Others collected exquisite and rare specimens to add to private and public gardens. With the interest in scientific inquiry in the eighteenth century, many plant hunters collected in pursuit of scientific knowledge. In the nineteenth century, plant hunters focused on searching for new varieties of fruits and grains and vegetables and trees and flowers to benefit farmers and gardeners and consumers.

In 1898, the United States Department of Agriculture

established an official plant exploration program that continues to this day. The Royal Botanic Garden in Edinburgh, Scotland, has an article on its Web site, "The Impact of the Plant-hunters," that begins with this tribute: "These intrepid explorers risked life and limb to bring back exotic plants for our gardens from far-off places. Their collections made a profound, and often under-acknowledged contribution not just to our gardens, but to our culture and lifestyles, and to the very wealth of the nation."

Mary Gibson Henry became a plant hunter because she could not obtain the plants that she wanted from commercial or botanic gardens in America or Europe. So, she set out to get them herself. She was forty-four years old. "It was 19 years after I was married before I had a whole 'day off' by myself without a member of my family," she wrote. "No one appreciated this long term of home duty more than my husband did and he showed his appreciation by saying, 'Go to it and go to all the places and do all the things you want to do and I believe are well fitted to do. You have earned it all.'"

She had her own car and a driver. Sometimes her husband came along, sometimes her whole family. The car was fitted with a bookcase, an electrically lit desk, and a rear compartment that was "insulated and ventilated so the newly collected plants travel comfortably." There was an assortment of equipment, including buckets, spades, a sheath knife, three plant presses for making herbaria (dried specimens for scientific study), notebooks and pencils to record detailed information about the specimen and its habitat, and cans to carry live specimens.

"My first real plant collecting trip," Henry wrote, "was taken in order to obtain a few specimens of *Rhododendron speciosum*, described so glowingly in Bartram's *Travels*. My journey of approximately 2500 miles in a car, and many on foot, was eminently successful."

That was just the beginning. Over the next forty years, the indomitable and exuberant Mary Henry made countless expeditions, going deep into swamps and forests, across rivers, through meadows, and up and over mountains.

"Countless Rattlesnake-Infested Swamps"

Her first trips were up and down the Atlantic Coast. "I soon learned," she wrote,

that rare and beautiful plants can only be found in places that are difficult of access. . . . Often one has to shove one's self through or wriggle under briars, with awkward results to clothing and many deep cuts and scratches. Tramps through lonely, pathless forests are often the means to an end. Wading, usually barelegged, through countless rattlesnake-infested swamps adds immensely to the interest of the day's work. On several occasions I have been so deeply mired I had to be pulled out. Wearing hip boots in the summer in states bordering the Gulf of

Mexico is not practical. It is too hot and the swamps are often deeper than the boots are high.

Henry expanded her explorations into the Piedmont Plateau, the region of low, rolling hills between the coast and the Appalachian Mountains. "The eastern slopes of these mountains were so beautiful and so enormously interesting," she wrote, "that I spent numerous seasons among them. In this wild and rugged country I had many adventures." Once, when she and her daughter Josephine were deep in the woods, they were held up and "roughly" threatened by three men with rifles. "It all took place so quickly we felt as though we were at the movies," Henry recalled. "I had often wondered how it would feel to be held up and really it was not bad at all."

A trapper's story led to Henry's daring expeditions to the "Blind Spot" of Canada, so called because of the formidable obstacles to travelers—waterfalls and rapids, mountainous wilderness country, long stretches where instead of firm ground there was muskeg, a soggy, seemingly bottomless black peat bog, and many "blank spots," or unmapped areas.

Henry was camping with her family in Jasper, British Columbia, in Canada, when the trapper told them about a valley with hot springs, also called a "tropical valley," near the Laird River in northern British Columbia. Although they were skeptical because that region was surrounded by ice and snow, with winter temperatures that plunged way below zero, Henry and her family were intrigued. Her husband and four children, who ranged in age from fourteen to twenty-one, "wanted to go for the adventure, plus hunting and fishing." She was "anxious to collect plants" for her own experimental garden as well as the Royal Botanic Garden in Edinburgh, Scotland, and the Academy of Natural Sciences in Philadelphia.

"A Perilous Journey"

"We were advised not to undertake such a perilous journey," she wrote, "but the more difficulties that arose, the more we wanted to go." They planned for nine months—scrutinizing maps and reports from the Canadian government, identifying unmapped areas, learning about the men who died while trying to cross that region during the gold rush of 1898. On June 25, 1930, they left Philadelphia and traveled by train and car and ferry to Fort St. John on the Peace River in British Columbia, the place where civilization ended. That is where their outfitter met them there with nine men, fifty-eight horses, tents, food, and other supplies, and they were joined by K. F. McCusker, Canada's foremost topographer, who was going along to map the mountainous wilderness they planned to explore.

On July 1, they headed out on horseback. Henry's horse, Chum, was a strong, black animal and big, so big that Henry, who was small, had to stand on her tiptoes to fasten her equipment—saddlebags with empty tin cans for plants, plant press, rifle, fishing rod, camera, field glasses, trowel, knife, slicker, and coat—to his saddle. "There was scarcely room for me," she wrote.

They rode fifteen to twenty miles a day. Once a week or so, they stopped a day to rest the horses. On those days Henry usually climbed a mountain. McCusker went with her to get information for the maps that he worked on every night, while they all sat around the campfire. Oftentimes they listened to the sounds of music from a hand-cranked Victrola, or record player. "A

Mary Gibson Henry at Caribou Pass in northern British Columbia. She is holding a plant press. Her camera equipment is in the saddlebag, a fishing pole and rifle are in a scabbard on the side of the saddle.

Victrola is at its best," Henry wrote, "with a camp fire in the foreground and black darkness beyond, and even an ordinary, everyday melody sounded wonderfully lovely in the calm shade of a tall fir tree or the purple shadow of a mountainside."

It was the time of year of long days, when the sun rose very early and set very late. Most nights the temperature plunged below zero, freezing the bathing suits that they wore during the day to go swimming, and their shoes, which they wore to ford river after river. At night they slept in canvas tents. Henry, who shared a tent with Josephine and Mary, was delighted that her daughters wanted to keep the tent flap "thrown wide back all night . . . it was so glorious to look out and watch the morning come." After a few nights, they decided not to put the inflatable mattresses under their sleeping bags. "It may not sound very comfortable, but we found it so," Henry wrote. "Of course when the ground was *very* rough we sometimes arose with our bodies slightly bruised, which really mattered not at all."

Henry's youngest child, fourteen-year-old Howard, loved to fish and hunt, and he and the others provided Jack, the cook, with fish and game for breakfast and dinner. For lunch they had sandwiches, which they usually ate while they rode.

"Bits of Fallen Sky"

"For the first few weeks we rode along rivers and through meadows," Henry wrote. "The flowers were simply marvelous. Polemoniums, Delphiniums, Mertensias and Penstemons grew in undreamed of profusion. We rode for miles and miles through meadows so blue they looked like bits of fallen sky. I never imagined meadows could be so gloriously beautiful."

Whether Henry was on horseback or on foot, she was always plant hunting. Each morning she put empty cans in the saddlebags that she attached to the pommel of her saddle. "Whenever I saw a plant I wanted, during our ride, I dismounted, dug it up, slipped it into a can and then caught up with others as fast as Chum, my horse, could carry me," she wrote. She also collected plants and flowers to put in her plant press to make dried specimens. Every evening Henry tended to her collections. She organized her pressed specimens and "aired and watered" the live plants. In the morning she packed the cans full with live plants into wooden packing cases that were strapped to the pack horses. "Sometimes the cans were frozen solid to the ground and I had to use my ax to chop them loose," she wrote. Two-thirds of the plants would not survive the strenuous trip, but the ones that did provided invaluable information about the region.

Heading in a northwesterly direction, they traveled toward the mountains. "The grandeur of the scenery, the lavishness of nature and the beauty of the flowers, daily quite took my breath away," Henry wrote. "Frequently I led my horse nearly all day that I might be close as possible to the glorious carpet that covered the earth. . . . Each day seemed to bring a new thrill of some sort." Some thrills were spectacular, such as the sight of "hillsides where thousands upon thousands of roses were abloom in such quantities they made the landscape quite pink and perfumed the air for miles with their delicious fragrance."

Crossing deep, fast-flowing rivers was a source of thrills, too. At the Muskwa River, the guides built two rafts to transport the supplies. Henry and her family chose to ride their horses across—a dangerous undertaking. "We preferred to swim our horses," Henry wrote. "After some urging they entered the water rather bravely, but when the deep, fast current swept them off their feet it took a bit of their nerve. Of course this method of crossing a river is always an exciting performance, and we enjoyed it thoroughly." Henry kept an eye on her family while crossing on Chum, who was a good swimmer. "For 58 horses in the water swimming together created quite a confusion. It was with real satisfaction that I saw them here and there in the water, and making good progress."

As for the muskegs, everyone dreaded them. One was so bad, Henry reported, "We really did not go *over* it, we literally went *through* it, wading, wallowing, and stumbling through it. . . . After Chum bogged down until almost half his body was in mud, I got off at every bad place to try and help him through these terrible mires." Many times horses had to be hauled out with ropes, and once a horse could not be saved.

"Nothing Else Mattered"

By mid-July, they were riding high above the timberline, the elevation beyond which trees will not grow. They had followed trails made by Indians, then trails made by game—grizzly bears, elk, mountain sheep, caribou, wolves. Sometimes there was no trail at all, and they relied solely on their compass. As they approached Caribou Pass, with an altitude of 6,500 feet, new flowers appeared. Henry spied a large "pure, pale, almost skyblue" flower with "a gorgeous orange throat. . . . The petals seemed to be made of a delicate semi-diaphanous substance and were all crinkly at the margins. The leaves were fine, like those of a small fern, and the tiny leaflets were strung along the stems like little green beads." She was transfixed: "Nothing else mattered, and when I looked up at last the others, with their horses in the distance looked like ants! . . . I gathered, ever so tenderly, these most appealing blossoms and placed them in my press, and then continued on my way to the summit of the pass."

Very early in the morning of August 5, Henry saw "the most beautiful snow covered mountain I had ever seen. . . . A great 9,000-foot pile, crowned with ice and snow." McCusker said it was an unmapped mountain. He mapped it and named it Mount Mary Henry, a decision later made official by the Canadian government.

The next day they happened upon a camp of Sikanni Indians. The chief's son, Charlie, knew where the "tropical valley" was, and agreed to lead them through the wild and desolate region that lay ahead. The way followed along the Tetsa River, where Howard caught huge trout, up to St. Paul's Lake, down into the valley of McDonnell Creek, on to where the Racing River, the fastest-running river they had ever seen, joined the Toad River, where the water was "a beautiful very deep sea green color . . . clear and transparent."

Leaving their horses with the outfitter, they rowed across the river in their little inflatable boat, "tossed like a cork on the fast and turbulent waters." The mysterious valley was close by. The path was clear, until they encountered a patch of burned and fallen trees, strewn about like pick-up sticks. They had no choice but to walk on the rotten tree trunks, sometimes six feet above a tangle of logs. "Several times, I landed on the ground after bumping on the logs beneath as I fell," Henry wrote. Finally they reached their goal.

The small valley was indeed tropical, full of springs with hot, even boiling water. As for rare plants to collect, Henry wrote, "My heart sank, for I saw that the valley it had taken us thirty-nine days to reach, had been devastated by fire. . . . So if the 'Tropical Valley' was not all, in my great enthusiasm, I hoped it would be, the marvelous scenery and transcending beauty of the flowers every day this summer made the trip vastly worthwhile."

Two days later, they headed home. "To be honest," Henry wrote, "I must admit I did not want to turn homeward. Our trip had all been so wonderful and so interesting that I should have liked to have kept on going indefinitely, not caring where I went so long as I was in the mountains and heading north."

Charlie went back with them as far as his people's camp. "By this time," Henry wrote, "we considered him one of our best friends."

"We Were So Cold"

The days were shorter now, and the weather changeable. On one particularly miserable day, they rode eleven hours in a cold downpour. Henry's hands were so cold and numb she had trouble holding her trowel when she dug up plants. Twice they got snowed in, but even worse weather awaited them at Caribou Pass—a blizzard. Hoping to fight off the cold by walking,

Henry and most of the others led their horses up the pass. "We went with a sort of dogged determination . . . walking right into the teeth of the gale and we were so cold," she wrote, "we could hardly speak, and the snow continued to fall."

One step after another, they kept climbing. Finally they made it up and over and down, beyond the snow, into a meadow. Mounting their horses, they rode ahead, grateful to see the sun and feel its "delicious life-giving warmth."

On September 17, they reached Hudson's Hope, a little town on the Peace River. Their eighty-day, thousand-mile journey was over. Henry had collected fifty cans of living plants for her experimental garden, gathered seventy-six packages of seeds, and made a herbarium collection for the Royal Botanic Garden in Edinburgh, Scotland, and the Academy of Natural Sciences in Philadelphia.

The thought of leaving Chum "really hurt" Mary Henry. "We had struggled over many, many weary but happy miles together, through heat and cold, and storm and sunshine. Chum, dear Chum," she wrote, "I put my face against his soft black cheek and kissed his nose good-bye."

A year later, Mary Henry had "a great longing" for the wilderness and so she returned to the Northland. Her daughter Josephine joined her. It was a short trip—five weeks—but they rode 460 miles and climbed seven mountains. McCusker went with them, plus Jack, the cook; Smoky, the horse wrangler; Ben, the Indian guide; and twenty-one horses, including Chum. Henry was overjoyed to see Chum and "could hardly wait to

Mary Gibson Henry and Josephine.

feel his big black body swaying beneath me as, covering mile after mile, we wended our way into the mountains." One day, Jo, who was collecting insects, asked Smoky if he had seen her mother. "No," Smoky replied, "but her horse is coming with a lot of shrubbery and I suppose she is behind it."

The next year she returned again to "that magnificent country where . . . the sky is the only ceiling and the floor is a grassy carpet." Jo was with her, so was McCusker, four other men, and twenty-four horses, with Belle substituting for Chum who was off on another trip. They headed north, and that night, Henry "slept as I love to sleep, with Mother Earth for my bed." In forty-one days, they covered 491 miles on horse and foot and mapped another "blank spot." Although Henry's heart "sang with joy," it was a trip of misfortunes, including four snowstorms, the near drowning of three men, and the loss of a raft with 450 pounds of food in a tumultuous river. "Maybe there were some rough spots," she wrote, "but we had an exciting and successful trip and a perfectly wonderful time." The last night they camped on the bank of the Peace River. "I watched the moon rise slowly from behind the distant jet black mountain," Henry wrote, "and somehow I knew that one day I would return."

Two years later, in 1935, Mary Henry's "old longings for the Northland returned a hundredfold," and she undertook her longest trip yet—1,200 miles in ninety days—across the unmapped wilderness to Alaska. She had discussed her route with the Sikanni Indians, and they said it could be done. Jo accompanied her, as did McCusker, who would, as before, map the country. To keep in touch with her husband, Henry brought along a receiving set, and every two weeks at 12:55 A.M. (the best time to receive messages), she listened for the words "calling Mrs. Henry somewhere in the Northwest Territory." It was, she wrote, "the most exciting address I ever had and always thrilled me to the core." To send messages out, Henry brought along twelve carrier pigeons, the only way to transmit messages to her husband from such remote areas.

"The Wolves Howled"

Once again, Henry "rode along rivers and through forests and over marvelous blue meadows and sometimes when the wind blew they appeared like the waves of the sea. . . . Often at night the wolves howled about our tents, truly the 'call of the wild' and I loved these eerie sounds."

Henry and Jo provided the food they needed. They fished, and once Henry caught a thirty-two-and-a-half-inch lake trout. They shot bears, mountain sheep, deer, and mountain goats with their rifles, and grouse with their pistols. "September 13th I left camp early to hunt and before long I saw a bear which I was lucky enough to kill with one shot," Henry wrote. "That day Jo, too, killed a bear, evidently Friday the 13th is an unlucky day for bears."

On this trip the horses were a problem. Henry's horse, Sunny, threw her five times. Once Sunny "fell over sideways" on a mountainside. Jo witnessed the scene and reported that her mother "just managed to keep a half a somersault ahead of him." Then Henry watched Jo's horse fall over a ridge. "My heart nearly stood still as together they fell and disappeared out of sight. They landed about 20 feet below on deep lichen covered rocks. Mercifully she and the horse were none the worse. The men too were thrown at various times."

Henry took a backpacking trip to get a close look at Mount Mary Henry. McCusker and another man, Glen, went with her. "We had no tent," she wrote, "and it was fun sleeping under the sky even though it was blackened by an approaching storm and the snow soon came down on my face." McCusker got sick and had to stay in camp while Henry and Glen "tramped over sixty miles and twice climbed to 8,000 feet in three days, saw sheep and caribou and faced a pack of wolves and had a perfectly marvelous time." After three days, they rejoined the rest of their group.

They survived several blizzards, and finally reached their destination, Wrangell, Alaska, on October 2. "The happy days in the wilderness had passed all too quickly," Henry wrote. "The best in life is only to be had by contrast and we enjoy good times a hundredfold when hard work brings them to us."

That was Henry's last trip to the Northland, although she continued to explore and hunt plants in other places—Bolivia and Honduras; the mountains of New Mexico, Oklahoma, and Arkansas; and the swamps of Virginia, North Carolina, Louisiana, Mississippi, and Texas. She particularly liked the Georgia swamps. "Georgia has the most beautiful azaleas in the world," she once told a reporter. And she added, "Marvellous snakes there!"

Mary Gibson Henry discovered and described more than fifty new botanical species, including the first new species of native American lily in more than one hundred years and a hundred-foot species of swamp cedar. During the winter months, she focused on what she called her "winter fun," and experimented with breeding new plants in her greenhouse. Over the years, she raised many new hybrids, including a "race of summer blooming Azaleas that flower the end of July and early August." Henry published articles and lectured in America and Great Britain. She received several honors for her work—the Mungo Park Medal from the Royal Scottish Geographical Society, the Schaffer Gold Medal from the Pennsylvania Horticultural Society, the Herbert Medal from the American Plant Life Society (now called the International Bulb Society). Many of the plants she discovered include her Latinized last name, such as *Chamaecyparis henryae*—the Atlantic white cedar.

Mary Gibson Henry had a heart attack and died in 1967 while on a plant-hunting expedition in North Carolina. "As for the flowers," she once wrote, "although many and many a time I risked my life for them, the flowers have done far more for me than I have done for them."

CHAPTER THREE

"A Preeminent Woman"

JUANA BRIONES:
ENTERPRISING FAMILY HEAD

1802–1889

There are no photographs of Juana Briones, only this drawing that was based on the appearance of one of Briones's relatives who was said to resemble her.

JUANA BRIONES lived during a time when it was extremely difficult, if not impossible, for a woman to do what she had to do, but she did it anyhow. She had married Apolinario Miranda, a cavalryman stationed at the military garrison, El Presidio de San Francisco, in the Spanish colony called Alta California (now California). Together they had eleven children, four of whom died in childhood. Seven survived: Presentación, called Concepción or Encarnación; Tomás; Narcisa; Refugio; José de Jesús Julian; Manuela; José Aniceto, usually called Dolores.

By law and tradition, Apolinario was the head of the family, and he was expected to provide for Juana and their children; instead he drank heavily. Juana, who could not read or write, set about providing for her family.

Alta California underwent great changes during Juana Briones's lifetime. Having started out as Indian country, it was a colony of Spain when Juana was born. Then Alta California became a province of Mexico, then a part of the United States, and—in 1850—it became the thirty-first state, California, and changed official languages from Spanish to English. The discovery of gold in 1848 set off the Gold Rush that transformed trading posts and villages into jam-packed cities, resounding with the hubbub and hullabaloo of fortune seekers. The population exploded to well over one hundred thousand by the end of 1849.

Juana was born in 1802 in Branciforte, now called Santa Cruz. Her parents had been born in Mexico. Her mother, Ysadora Tapia, was four years old when she and her family joined an expedition that traveled 1,600 miles overland from Mexico to settle in Alta California. Her father, Marcos Briones, was a soldier who was primarily stationed at Monterey Presidio. Juana and her sisters Guadalupe, María de la Luz (called Luz), and Epicacia and her brothers José Antonio, Felipe, and Gregorio were *Californios*, the first generation of Spanish-speaking people to be born in California.

Juana grew up in close contact with Indians, the native Californians and the majority population at that time. From the

Indians and her mother and her elder sister Guadalupe, Juana learned how various herbs could cure sick people and heal wounds, and other secret remedies, including the benefits of mud baths.

Juana's mother died in 1812, and her father, Marcos, moved the family to El Polin Spring, near El Presidio de San Francisco. That is where Juana eventually met Apolinario and got married in 1820. At first, they may have lived with her father in his house. Then they went to live with her sister Guadalupe and her husband, Candelario Miramontes, in the house Guadalupe and Candelario built next to Marcos's house.

"Stowed Us Away"

In 1833, Apolinario petitioned for a grant of property called Ojo de Agua de Figueroa that had a spring and a stream running though the middle of it. Their first house, a *palizada*, or stockade, was soon replaced by an adobe house. The property was fenced and had a corral. Here was where Juana Briones started her enterprises to provide for her family. She tended to the fruit trees and vegetables and raised cattle and chickens and other livestock. Over the years, increasing numbers of ships came to San Francisco Bay, and the sailors were eager to buy Briones's fresh produce.

Sailors who "jumped ship," or ran away to escape horrific conditions, sought her help, and she would protect them until their ship left port and they were safe. Many years after Briones helped him, one sailor, Charles Brown, told this story: "An old lady named Juana Briones residing in the Presidio, understanding that myself, Ephrian P. Farwell, Gregorio Escalante (a Manila man) and an Indian, named Elijah . . . wanted to run, stowed us away in the loft of her house; from there she moved Farwell and me to the bushes on Black Pt. Then she sent for her brother, Felipe Briones, from Pinole, who came and carried us over there. . . . Elijah . . . sat on a limb of a tree, which he cut off, fell and broke his jaw. Juana Briones cured him."

In the mid-1830s, Juana Briones decided to expand her enterprise and obtain a piece of property closer to the bay where the ships anchored.

Briones appeared unafraid to do business at a time when women, especially married women, had few legal rights. She also was undeterred by the fact that she could not read or write. Determinedly, Briones did what she had to do to provide for her family. She selected people she could trust to read and write for her. When she needed to sign personal or business documents, she signed with the mark of a cross. Her new property was in Yerba Buena, named for the good smelling herb that covered the hillsides, making her one of the first three residents of the settlement that would become San Francisco.

"She Feared No Disease"

Juana Briones had an adobe house built, planted a garden, raised cattle, milked her cows, and sold produce. Her neighbors and visitors and sick sailors sought her out because of her growing reputation as a *curandera*, a traditional healer. "The pioneers of the late 1830s and the travelers of the early 1840s seldom failed to mention this lady," wrote J. N. Bowman, a historian. "She feared no disease. Ships brought in men suffering from smallpox and scurvy and she took them in as readily as the mildest fever case. She said, 'I want no pay. If they get well, I am satisfied.'"

In some cases, Briones administered a mud bath. As one writer described it,

this consisted of a trench about five feet long, two feet wide and eighteen inches deep. Near this trench she had a huge kettle filled with water; when it was hot she stirred adobe mud into it. When the bath was ready the patient was brought out, stripped to the loin cloth, and laid upon a cowhide. Then the hot mud was poured over him by Madame Briones and her Indian girls. If the patient objected too strongly, his head and feet were held down. It is said that many cures were effected in this manner.

Briones was well-known for her hospitality. Visitors and dignitaries would stop by for a cup of mint tea made from yerba buena, the herb she gathered from the nearby hillsides. During holidays, she held memorable parties. One of her guests, an American businessman, recalled playing a game that involved cracking an eggshell filled with confetti or tinsel on someone's head, or trying to. Presentación, Juana's nineteen-year-old daughter, he reported, was too quick for him.

Briones so transformed the beach with her activities that before long it was named Playa de Juana Briones.

One sailor, W. H. Thomes, came to the bay in 1843 and later wrote about buying milk from Juana Briones, whom he referred to as Señora Abarono in his book *On Land and Sea*. (Abarono "is evidently an American spelling of Briones as it was pronounced locally," according to the historian J. N. Bowman. Baroma and Barona were other early spellings of Briones.)

Thomes described the view of her house from the top of Telegraph Hill: "In the rear of the town were vast sand mounds, ever changing, while at the foot of the hill, on the Golden Gate side, was a large adobe house, and outbuildings, the residence and rancho of Señora Abarono . . . where I afterward used to go for milk every morning, unless off on boating duty. The lady and I struck up quite a friendship. She always welcomed me with a polite good morning, and a drink of fresh milk."

"Lasso the Milking Cow"

Thomes and his shipmate French Lewey "climbed on top of an adobe wall" to observe "a real California milking operation; and it would have made a Vermont farmer wild to have seen the performance." Here are excerpts from Thomes's account:

Señora Abarono was already stirring when we reached her premises. Her shrill voice was heard from afar, scolding her servants, and urging them to do many things at the same time; yet, when she saw Lewey and me, she gave us a

smiling welcome, and pleasant good-morning, and inti-
mated that we were the best boys she had ever seen,
which was news to us, but exceedingly gratifying at the
same time, for we were just vain enough to like compli-
ments of that kind.

"Ah!" the good lady said, as she beamed on us, "you
want milk for the captain and cabin, do you? Well, you
shall have it. Pedro," she shrieked, "lasso the milking cows,
and be quick about it."

Pedro did not seem to think that there was any occasion
of haste, but he took his *riata* [lasso] and started for the
corral where a dozen wild-eyed cows, and their calves
were confined and looked dangerous to approach. . . .

Pedro did not seem to have any fear of the cattle. He
entered the corral, regardless of horn and heels, selected a
cow, threw his lasso over her head, and dragged her out of
the pen, in spite of plunges and bellowings, and the shrill
bleating of her calf. Then Pedro put up the bars, so that
the stock could not escape, took a turn with his *riata*
around a stout stump, dragged the plunging animal up to
it, made all fast, and then secured the cow's hind legs, and
tail, with a lashing of rawhide, thus insuring some gentle
milkmaid from being kicked clear through the adobe wall,
and into the adjoining waters of the Golden Gate, for a
cross California cow could kick like a mule, and fight like
a bull, when so disposed. . . .

The lady . . . squatted at the side of the cow. The animal gave a bellow, and made desperate attempts to kick, but could not do so owing to the stout lashings on the hind legs. Then the Señora plunged at the teats, but the cow was stubborn and refused to give down a drop of milk, and her eyes looked threatening, as she humped her back for a mighty leap. But the lady only smiled and scolded. She knew her business.

"Get the calf loose, Pedro," she said, and the muzzle was taken from the struggling, impatient offspring, and, with a glad bleat, it ran to its mother, butted her, tugged at her teats, and the obstinate feelings of the cow were overcome. Her eyes lost some of their wildness, her bucking ceased and with a bellow of satisfaction, she gave down milk, and the calf commenced to gorge itself, but just at this point Pedro stepped in, pulled away the glutton, and the lady took its place, and milked the unruly creature with perfect composure, or until the supply was exhausted, and then another cow was treated in the same way, and the first one was turned loose to the grazing grounds of the rancho, and so on until half a dozen had been milked.

We were gratified by seeing our milk come . . . and we bottled it with a grin of satisfaction. . . . We thanked the bright, vivacious Señora and promised to come the next day, and get a fresh supply of milk, and we also agreed to give Pedro half a dozen cakes of ship-bread, something he was anxious to taste.

"*By the Labor of My Own Hands*"

In the early 1840s, Apolinario's behavior got worse, and Juana appealed to civil and military authorities for help. Despite receiving several reprimands, Apolinario continued to trouble Juana and the eight children, who now included Cecilia Chohuihuala, an orphaned Indian girl whom Briones had adopted.

Divorce was not legal, but the bishop could issue a church-sanctioned separation. In 1844, Briones asked a priest to write her petition addressed to Bishop Francisco García Diego y Moreno in Santa Barbara: "I fear the destruction of my unfortunate family due to the scandal and bad example of a man who has forgotten God, and his own soul, whose only concern is drunkenness and all the vices that come with it, and who no longer cares about feeding his family, a burden that I alone carry with the labor of my own hand, a fact that I can prove with testimonials of exceptional strength if necessary. . . . Your Lordship, my husband is the greatest obstacle placed before my children, because of him they learn nothing but swearing, blasphemy, and ugly, lewd, and dissolute behavior. How will I excuse myself before God, if I do not seek, as much as I can, all possible means of ridding my family of such a bad example?"

There is no record of whether the bishop granted Briones's

Juana Briones's adobe house, Rancho la Purisima Concepción, about 1900.

request. However he did write to the *alcalde*, or the mayor, explaining Briones's situation and saying that something needed to be done. Whatever was done, it worked because Apolinario Miranda disappeared from Briones's life.

In 1844, Juana Briones set out to buy more land. This time it was the Rancho la Purisima Concepción, a 4,400-acre ranch in what is now Palo Alto and Los Altos, California. To do that she needed the governor's permission because she was a woman. "Being burdened with a large family and having a considerable amount of stock, cattle and horses, and needing a tract of land on which to place said stock," she asked her agent to write to the governor, "I pray you to be pleased to give me permission to purchase the same, and also to the owner leave to sell it."

The governor agreed, and Juana Briones bought Rancho la Purisima Concepción for three hundred dollars. She built a large adobe house with three oblong rooms (part of which still stands today) on the top of a hill, as well as several other buildings. Within two years, she had packed her possessions and furniture in oxcarts and saddled horses for herself and her children and moved to the ranch, a trip of three days. A man who once stayed at the ranch wrote that the quarters were "quite comfortable." He noted the presence of a number of Briones's children and Indians and "two little pet pigs in the cook house, and 15 or 20 dogs."

Apolinario died in 1847 and under Mexican law Juana inherited Ojo de Agua de Figueroa, which was in his name. However, in 1850, when Mexico ceded California to the United States, Briones and anyone else who bought land when California belonged to Spain or Mexico had to prove before a Land Commission, set up by the U.S. government, that their titles were legal, a complicated and costly process. Using *diseños* (hand-drawn maps), and calling many witnesses who testified that she owned the land, Briones did what many Spanish-speaking landowners were unable to do. After twelve years of legal wranglings, she won and kept both Ojo de Agua de Figueroa and Rancho la Purisima Concepción.

"She Liked Horses and Cattle"
Throughout this time, she continued to run her ranch. She regularly took oxcarts piled high with cowhides to San Francisco

and exchanged the hides for supplies. The trip took seven days and required getting a fresh team of oxen three times each way.

Juana Briones continued to buy and sell property, and eventually sold her Yerba Buena and Ojo de Agua properties, paying attention to every detail of each transaction. As she had for her whole life, she provided for her family's future, and she carefully divided up her land among her children. She continued to care for sick people. When an epidemic of smallpox, a contagious and deadly disease, broke out in Bolinas, she went there to help. There is a legend that she even tended to a famed bandit, Joaquin Murietta, when he was wounded. Supposedly Murietta buried his booty on her ranch where, so the story goes, it still remains.

Once a year, Juana Briones held a barbecue at the ranch. Her children and their families came for the festivities, which lasted several days. Her sister Guadalupe and her family came from Half Moon Bay with their musical instruments and formed their own band. Finally, when Juana Briones was in her mid-eighties, she moved to Mayfield, California, and spent the rest of her life in a frame house she built on a lot between two of her daughters, Manuela and Refugio, although she missed her ranch. "She liked horses and cattle and everything that goes with ranching," her grandson remembered.

"She Straightened to Her Full Height"

There are no pictures of Juana Briones, only a sketch done by an artist based on a picture of a niece who resembled Briones.

Her grandson described her as being "very tall for a woman, fair in complexion, her hair parted in the middle with a long string of black beads around her neck." He recalled that "her voice was low and she spoke slowly even dragging her words. . . . In her later days she was slightly stooped and walked with a long staff; but when she was angry she straightened to her full height, her eyes flashed, and she bore the dignity of a Spanish doña."

Juana Briones died on December 3, 1889. She was buried on a very rainy day next to her sister Luz. No stone marks her grave, although her grandson said she was buried in the southeast corner of the lot just west of the plot marked Greer, near the entrance of Holy Cross Cemetery, Menlo Park, California.

In 2003 a team of archaeologists led by Dr. Barbara Voss discovered the stone foundation of Marcos Briones's house, where Juana most likely would have lived from the time she was ten years old and even, for a while, after she got married. The house was on El Presidio de San Francisco land that was a U.S. army base for many years and is now a national park. It is an open site, meaning that the public can visit it on weekdays during the summer and watch the archaeologists work and ask questions.

Juana Briones lived an adventurous life as a rancher, healer, businesswoman, land owner, and provider for her family. Her legacy is alive today in the spirit of children who attend the

Plaque commemorating Juana Briones y Tapia de Miranda in Washington Square Park, San Francisco, California.

Juana Briones Elementary School in Palo Alto, California, and in words on the Washington Square Park state historic marker in the North Beach area of San Francisco. Dedicated in 1997, the plaque is the first to honor a woman in San Francisco:

JUANA BRIONES Y TAPIA DE MIRANDA

1802–1889

NORTH BEACH PIONEER

JUANA BRIONES, BORN IN HISPANIC CALIFORNIA, WAS A PREEMINENT WOMAN OF HER TIME. IN THE 1830S AND 1840S SHE TRANS-FORMED AN ISOLATED COVE IN THE THEN MEXICAN HAMLET OF

YERBA BUENA INTO HER RANCHO. AT THE SITE OF THIS PARK SHE RAISED CATTLE AND GREW VEGETABLES FOR SALE TO SHIP CREWS. SHE GAVE SANCTUARY TO REFUGEES AND WAS REVERED AS A HEALER AND CARE-GIVER. SHE IS HONORED AS A HUMANITARIAN, ASTUTE BUSINESSWOMAN, COMMUNITY BUILDER, AND DEVOTED MOTHER OF EIGHT CHILDREN.

CHAPTER FOUR

"Great Clouds of Yellow and Orange Fumes"

ALICE HAMILTON: SUPERSLEUTH

1869–1970

ALICE HAMILTON wanted to be a medical doctor. Her sister told her that was a "disgusting" idea. When she expressed a desire to observe an operation, a teacher told her that she was "a bluggy-minded butcher." But Alice was undeterred. "As a doctor," she said, "I could go anywhere I pleased—to far-off lands or to city slums—and be quite sure that I could be of use anywhere."

Alice was right, although she could hardly have predicted that she would spend much of her career going to places filled with poisons, a far cry from her growing-up years in Fort Wayne, Indiana, a small, quiet city where elm and maple trees lined the streets. Three families of Hamiltons lived on the same block in three big houses—the Old House (built in 1840), the Red House (made of brick), and the White House (a frame house where Alice lived). Alice, a lissome girl with big, expressive dark eyes and light brown hair, and her three sisters and eleven cousins spent their days inventing games, going for long

Left to right: Norah, Margaret, Alice, and Edith

Left to right:
Alice, Allen, and Agnes

"The three A's" and the Hamilton sisters.

walks, finding "endless hiding places in lilac hedges or up in the thick leaves of an apple tree," and "talking about everything." Throughout her life, Alice was closely connected to her sisters Edith, Margaret, and Norah, and two of her cousins. She and these cousins—Agnes and Allen—were just months apart in age, and dubbed themselves "the three A's."

As for school, Alice's parents did not send their children. The school day lasted too long, their mother thought. Their father thought there was too much arithmetic and American history in the curriculum. Alice and her siblings learned languages and literature and history from their parents, an occasional tutor, and from their own reading, but they learned little science. "Yet," Alice said, "in a way we were trained in habits of the scientific approach. We were not allowed to make a statement which could be challenged unless we were prepared to defend it."

When she was seventeen years old, Alice finally went to school—Miss Porter's School in Farmington, Connecticut, the school her aunts and sisters and cousins attended. "The teaching," Alice remembered, "was the world's worst." What was good was meeting other girls from different backgrounds, taking two-hour walks every afternoon, and being influenced by Miss Sarah Porter herself. "She gave us," Alice wrote, "somehow the best of the New England tradition—integrity, self-control, no weakness or sentimentality, love of beauty, respect for the intellectual, clear thinking, no nonsense."

Alice added these lessons to her mother's message that "personal liberty was the most precious thing in life." Equally instructive for Alice was her mother's "capacity for enthusiasm and indignation over events and causes . . . tales of police brutality, of the lynching of Negroes, over child labor and cruelty to prisoners. . . . She made us feel that whatever went wrong in our society was a personal concern for her and for us."

After two years at Miss Porter's, Alice Hamilton returned to Fort Wayne with the "hope of a wide and full life, of going out into the big world," a world that in the 1890s had more opportunities for women than ever before. Deciding to study medicine, Hamilton made up for her "incomplete and scrappy" education by studying science—physics, chemistry, and anatomy—first with a high school teacher and then at a local medical school. Then she entered the Medical School of the University of Michigan, a school that was both a pioneer in admitting women and in providing modern medical training. "Those were very happy and exciting years," she wrote. "I shall never forget the revelation that came to me when I saw through the microscope the cells which make up the human body, and realized that later on I should be looking at these cells changed by disease—that the actual process of disease can be viewed by the human eye."

"Just Walk Fast"

Hamilton graduated from medical school and continued her studies in bacteriology, the study of tiny one-celled organisms, and pathology, the study of diseases, at the universities of Leipzig and Munich in Germany and at the Johns Hopkins University in Baltimore, Maryland. She also did an internship at a hospital in Boston, Massachusetts, and spent many nights going on calls to treat patients in different parts of the city, in saloons and houses of prostitution. "Each new call was an adventure," she said.

The first night Hamilton went out on a call, she got lost and later wrote:

[I] dared not ask help of any of the men who passed me but presently a little woman came hurrying along and I stopped her. She was very kind. She led me back to my street and laughed at my fears. She was a chorus girl, she told me, and she never had any trouble. "Just walk along fast with your bag in your hand, not looking at anybody, and nobody will speak to you. Men don't want to be snubbed; they are look- ing for a woman who is will- ing." It was good advice and it worked.

Alice Hamilton, 25, the year she graduated from medical school.

One of the other interns was named Rachelle Slobodinskaya. Born in Russia, she had been a revolutionary by the time she was thirteen, escaped to America when she was seventeen, and eked out a living working in sweatshops in New York City before managing to go to medical school. "She seemed to me the most exciting person I had ever met," Hamilton wrote. "In all my life I had never had to think where my next meal was coming from. Being so sheltered and so ignorant seemed contemptible."

In 1897, Hamilton was offered a job as professor of pathol- ogy at the Women's Medical School of Northwestern Univer- sity. "I accepted it with thankfulness, not only because it meant employment in my own field, but because it was in Chicago. At last I could realize the dream I had had for years of going to live in Hull House."

Hull House was a settlement house founded by Jane Addams and Ellen Gates Starr in 1889 in a working-class neighborhood on the West Side of Chicago, where recent immigrants— Italians, Serbians, Bulgarians, Hungarians, and Poles—lived packed together in unsanitary, often miserable, conditions. The immigrant women typically tended to their children and did piece-work for a pittance in their crowded, dilapidated wooden tenement houses. Many of the men worked under dangerous conditions in heavy industries—steel mills, factories that made railroad cars, and plants that processed lead. "The rule was," Hamilton wrote, "to work the men as hard as possible . . . pay them as low wages as possible, and then, when American ideas began to penetrate and revolt to raise its head, to put it down with force, discharge and blacklist the trouble-makers, and start afresh with a new lot of immigrants."

Idealistic, well-educated, white, middle- and upper-middle-class young women like Hamilton came to Hull House to participate in its two-way mission of improving the lives of the new immigrants *and* learning about the real world from them. Hull House offered many activities: a wide range of classes, such as English, music, and art; job training; lectures on social issues, politics, books, and history; day care, kindergarten, and after-school recreation; art exhibitions; and theater productions in Yiddish and in English.

"With Such Complete Sincerity"

Hamilton taught English, investigated the causes of tuberculosis and typhoid fever, fought against the cocaine trade, participated in picket lines, and started a baby clinic. "In settlement life," she wrote, "as one comes to know simple people intimately, one loses one's contempt for the banal, the bromide, the cliché, because one hears them used with such complete sincerity. You cannot laugh at 'There's nothing like a mother's love' when you hear it said by a widow who has made up her mind to turn scrubwoman in a downtown office rather than send her child to an orphanage." Settlement house life, Hamilton believed, taught people not to "divide people into sections and file them away in labelled cubby-holes, and think you know all about them."

In 1902, the Women's Medical School closed and Hamilton went to work as a bacteriologist in the laboratory at the Memorial Institute for Infectious Diseases. The work interested her, although she had self-doubts and wrote to her cousin that she would "never be more than a fourth-rate scientist." Even more distressing to her was the feeling that her laboratory work was disconnected from the real world of workers. How, she wondered, could she use her scientific knowledge to help people in practical ways?

An article and a book helped Hamilton find the answer to her question.

The article by William Hard, a young man with "a fiery pen," exposed an employer's negligence that had resulted in the death of a group of workers and the callous treatment of the workers' widows and children. The workers had been dropped off to work at an offshore water pumping station in Lake Michigan. When a fire broke out, they had no means of escape; their only choice was to either burn to death or drown. By the time a rescue boat arrived, most of the workers had drowned.

The book, *Dangerous Trades* by Sir Thomas Oliver, was a compendium of occupational diseases. Hamilton was particularly interested in Oliver's book because at Hull House she had heard "tales of the dangers that workingmen faced, a case of carbon-monoxide gassing in the great steel mills, of painters disabled by lead palsy, of pneumonia and rheumatism among the men in the stockyard."

As Hamilton knew, the dangers to workers were accidents and disease, especially diseases caused by industrial poisons. The ancient Romans and Greeks knew about the dangers of sulfide ores and carbon monoxide. Hippocrates described lead poisoning in the fifth century B.C.E. In the eleventh century, the Iranian physician Ibn Sina described the poisonous properties of arsenic trioxide. In the fifteenth century, Ulrich Ellenbog wrote the first printed book on industrial hazards and discussed lead and mercury. In the eighteenth century, Bernardino Ramazzini studied over fifty types of workers—miners, chemists, glassmakers, painters, tanners, sewage workers, printers—and recommended ways to reduce their risks of disease.

Galvanized by the article and book, Hamilton went "to the

Crerar Library to read everything I could on the dangers to industrial workers, and what could be done to protect them." To her surprise, she discovered that everything she read was "German, or British, Austrian, Dutch, Swiss, even Italian or Spanish—everything but American." Why not American, she wondered? Because, her medical friends told her, the working conditions in American factories were excellent. "That sort of talk always left me skeptical," Hamilton reported. Her "disbelief in the happy lot of American workers" was confirmed when she met John Andrews at Hull House and heard about his investigation that uncovered 150 cases of phossy jaw among workers in American match factories, disproving the widespread belief that there was no phossy jaw in America.

A horrendous disease, phossy jaw is caused by exposure to white or yellow phosphorus, a chemical used to make matches. The exposure can come from the fumes it gives off at room temperature or by getting it on something that ends up in a worker's mouth—fingers, food, gum, a drinking glass. In severe cases, workers must have one or both of their jawbones removed because of the abscesses that form. Andrews's investigation prompted the passage of a federal law that ended the use of phosphorus in American match factories. This success was part of a growing reform movement in America in the early 1900s to deal with numerous social and economic problems, including dangerous working conditions.

"Into a Great Unknown"

In 1908, the governor of Illinois appointed Alice Hamilton to a commission to study industrial diseases. It was the first investigation of this kind in the country. When the state legislature followed up by requesting a survey, Hamilton became the head of a team of twenty doctors, medical students, and social workers. "We were staggered by the complexity of the problem we faced," she wrote. "It was starting out into a great unknown."

Of the many industrial conditions that cause diseases—various dusts and fumes, temperature extremes, loud noise, heavy exertion—Hamilton's team decided to focus on poisons: lead, arsenic, brass, carbon monoxide, the cyanides, and turpentine. Each doctor selected a poison. Hamilton took lead, the most common industrial poison.

Lead is a slow-acting poison. It accumulates in a worker's body before attacking the digestive tract and blood system. Eventually it affects the nervous system ultimately resulting in "lead fits," or insanity. Although lead poisoning causes a variety of symptoms, early symptoms include pallor and sallowness, a metallic taste (especially in the morning), and an increasing loss of appetite. Workers with acute cases suffer from severe symptoms of colic, even convulsions, and palsy, or paralysis that typically begins in the wrist and develops into a condition known as "wrist-drop" because "the hand tends to fall and hang helplessly."

Hamilton knew the study would carry more weight if she

could "unearth actual instances of poisoning." To do that she had to understand the manufacturing process, figure out which industries used lead, and locate "leaded" workers. She and her assistants scrutinized hospital records and talked to labor leaders, doctors, apothecaries, chemists, and factory managers who routinely denied that any workers were sick. She went to workers' homes and visited 304 factories. She followed every clue, even ones based on gossip. "Thus," Hamilton wrote, "I was put on the trail of new lead trades, some of which I had never thought of—for instance, making freight-car seals, coffin 'trim,' and decalcomania papers for pottery decorations; polishing cut glass; brass founding; wrapping cigars in so-called tinfoil."

In the end, Hamilton located 578 affected workers. One was a thirty-six-year-old Hungarian who had worked for seven years grinding lead paint. "A skeleton of a man," she noted, "looking almost twice his age, his limbs soft and flabby, his muscles wasted . . . his color a dirty grayish yellow, his eyes dull and expressionless." She identified seventy industries that used lead. Most important, she proved that lead poisoning "is brought about far more rapidly and intensely by the breathing of lead-laden air than by the swallowing of lead."

"It was a pioneering exploration of an unknown field," Hamilton wrote. "Every article I wrote in those days, every speech I made, is full of pleading for the recognition of lead poisoning as a real and serious medical problem." A few months after Hamilton and her team presented their report, the Illinois

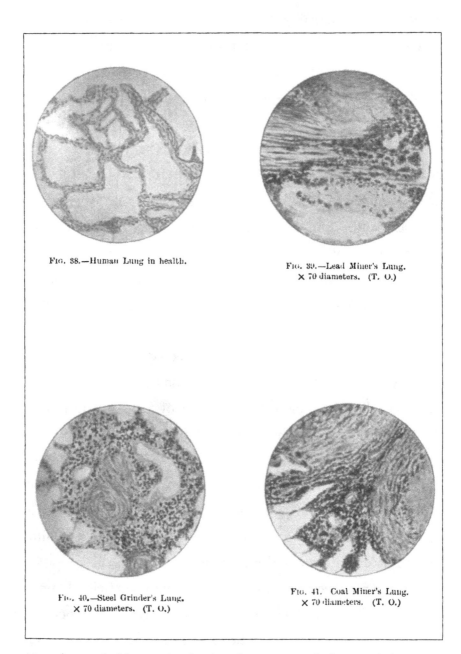

FIG. 38.—Human Lung in health.

FIG. 39.—Lead Miner's Lung.
× 70 diameters. (T. O.)

FIG. 40.—Steel Grinder's Lung.
× 70 diameters. (T. O.)

FIG. 41. Coal Miner's Lung.
× 70 diameters. (T. O.)

Microphotographs (photographs taken through a microscope of a lung sample that was examined after a person died) of a healthy human lung, a lead miner's lung, a steel grinder's lung, a coal miner's lung.

legislature passed an occupational disease law that included safety protections for workers and monthly medical examinations.

Alice Hamilton never returned to her job as a bacteriologist at the laboratory. "Interesting as I found the subject, and pleasant as I found the life, I was never absorbed in it," she wrote. Instead she agreed to conduct nationwide studies of poisonous trades for the federal government. "I never have doubted the wisdom of my decision to . . . devote myself to work which has been scientific only in part, but human and practical in greater measure," she wrote.

The terms of Hamilton's new job suited her. "The time devoted to each survey, that and all else, was left to my discretion," she wrote. "Nobody would keep tabs on me. I should not even receive a salary; only when the report was ready for publication would the government buy it from me at a price to be decided on." That fulfilled her desire for "personal liberty," but it also meant that she had no official status or help. Traveling alone, she had to figure out where the factories were, how to get inside, and what type of investigation to conduct. All this she had to do as a woman in the all-male environment of factories and in a country where women did not yet have the right to vote. Although she was described as "almost fragile," Hamilton calmly and determinedly proceeded, undeterred by "the tiresome tradition that a woman is something different and must be treated differently."

"Their Hair Was Full of It"

Her first assignment was to continue investigating the lead industry. Off she went to Nebraska, Colorado, Utah, Missouri, Illinois, Ohio, Pennsylvania, and New York. In St. Louis, Missouri, she inspected the worst factory she had ever seen. She discovered that most of the workers were "Negroes. . . . They were smeared with white-lead dust and their hair was full of it." One worker, who was pushing a wheelbarrow, "told me he had worked there a year and had had lead colic (he knew all about it) five times and that this was no unusual record. 'It is better pay than any other work a Negro can get, but it sure does break your health.' He gets $11.00 a week."

On a "bleak day in January, with a heavy, gray sky overhead, mud and slush underfoot," Hamilton arrived at Smelter Hill, Missouri, "the very dreariest, most hopeless community" she had ever seen, with "ramshackle, hastily built wooden houses, unpainted, sagging." The villagers who worked in the smelter, a factory that melts ore in order to get metal from it, were "hill people from the Ozarks or western Kentucky, or farmers from Arkansas; they were full of malaria, hookworm . . . to say nothing of lead." She discovered that they knew she was coming. "They've been cleaning up for you something fierce," one woman told her. "Why, in the room where my husband works they tore out the ceiling, because they couldn't cover up the red lead. And a doctor came and looked at all the men and them that's got lead, forty of them, has got to keep to home the day you're there."

Hamilton met the three owners "who waited for me to give them the praise they thought they deserved." In her polite but firm way, she told them that she knew about the cover-up. "So," she said, "I simply do not know what I can say in my report to Washington." The owners sat silently with guilty looks on their faces. "It was so funny," she wrote, "I could not help bursting out laughing, and as they all joined in, the situation lightened; they gaily admitted the fraud, and promised to let me see the doctor's report and to do everything they could to make the temporary reforms permanent, including regular medical examinations of the lead men."

Many years later, Hamilton visited the same factory and found better safety conditions and a much lower rate of lead poisoning. Sadly, she saw many new mines and "the same abomination of desolation in the countryside. . . . One village we visited might have been Smelter Hill in 1913, except the water peddler now drives a truck instead of a horse, and the people tell you about 'miner's con' [consumption, or wasting away of tissue] instead of lead colic." This disregard for workers and the environment, Hamilton felt, was the "seamy side of our American enterprise, our passion for progress."

Hamilton did more than write reports to bring about changes. She personally gave recommendations to managers and owners. When that was not enough, she found other ways.

In the case of the Pullman Company, where workers who painted the ceilings of railroad cars worked in extremely hazardous conditions, Hamilton contacted Mrs. Joseph T. Bowen, a strong supporter of Hull House and "a member of that all-too-small class of wealthy people who feel a direct responsibility toward the sources of their wealth." Bowen used her power as a important stockholder to pressure the managers. "Changes," Hamilton reported, "took place with breath-taking speed."

In the case of the Radium Girls, Hamilton enlisted Walter Lippmann, a popular columnist for the *New York World*, one of the most powerful newspapers in America. The Radium Girls were five women who had worked at the U.S. Radium Corporation in Orange, New Jersey. Dying of what they thought was radium poisoning, the women sued U.S. Radium. The company's owner denied that radium was dangerous. Hamilton and other experts knew that it was.

As the women's condition deteriorated, the company's lawyers stalled. Disgusted and infuriated, Alice Hamilton devised a public relations campaign and sought Lippmann's help. Using the scientific information Hamilton provided, Lippmann wrote a series of persuasive and passionate columns. The legal delays, he wrote were a "damnable travesty of justice. . . . The women are dying." In the face of growing public sympathy for the women and outrage toward U.S. Radium, the company finally settled. Each woman received ten thousand dollars, as well as a six-hundred-dollar annuity (yearly payment) for as long as she lived (which was not long). Hamilton continued working with Lippmann to call public attention to the dangers of radium and institute protection for workers.

"Clouds of Yellow and Orange Fumes"

Hamilton was investigating the rubber industry when World War I began and a new and rapidly expanding enterprise developed in the United States—the explosives industry. Hamilton was asked to investigate it.

"If there was anyone in Washington who knew where explosives were being produced and loaded . . . he kept the secret." So, Hamilton did what she had always done, "visit the plants I knew and pick up gossip about the others." She also followed the "great clouds of yellow and orange fumes, nitrous gases which . . . rose to the sky from picric-acid and nitrocellulose plants. . . . I would hear vaguely of a nitrating plant in the New Jersey marshes and I would spot the orange fumes and make my way to them. Sometimes it would be a group of 'canaries' who would guide me to a plant. These were men so stained with yellow picric acid that they were dubbed canaries."

The day she found a picric-acid plant in a meadow in New Jersey "with wide stretches of farmland about," she watched thick clouds of orange smoke rise and roll and sink and spread. The land was blackened, except for a "tiny mound covered with wild rose and morning-glory. The poison had not reached it yet, but was creeping close."

Suddenly the wind shifted and drove Hamilton "choking and gasping before the angry fumes which were pouring out again." Running toward clear air, Hamilton found herself in a field where corn used to grow. "It was better business," she wrote, "to work for destruction than for life and so the farmers had left the fields for the acid sheds, and instead of yellow corn to feed men their harvest was heaps of picric to kill men."

A pacifist, Alice Hamilton was open about her antiwar feelings. "It was not only the sight of men sickening and dying in the effort to produce something to wound or kill other men . . . but it was also the strange spirit of exaltation among the men and women who thronged Washington, engaged in all sorts of 'war work' and loving it. I got an impression of joyful release in many of them, as if, after all their lives repressing hatred as unchristian, they suddenly discovered it to be a patriotic duty and let themselves go in for an orgy of anti-German abuse."

During the war, Hamilton investigated one explosives plant after another. TNT plants that were built in remote narrow valleys to minimize the damage if they exploded. Mercury fulminate plants where she watched a workman carry a "great glass balloon" filled with thousands of highly volatile crystals. "I still shiver when I think of it," she wrote. Based on her investigations, Hamilton wrote reports and articles documenting the dangers, listing symptoms of poisoning, and recommending safety measures. She exchanged information with experts in Europe, who were ahead of the United States in instituting safety measures. In time, Hamilton was able to send well-trained medical students into the plants to do research. Gradually officials and employers and physicians began to pay attention.

By the end of the war, Hamilton said, "industrial medicine had at last become respectable."

After the war, Hamilton went to Arizona to investigate the copper mines. It was there that she had explored her first mine. Dressed in overalls and a helmet with a safety lamp, she descended eight hundred feet through the darkness in an elevator-type contraption called a cage. Stooped low, crawling on her hands and knees, and "climbing down an eighty-foot ladder into a black pit," she followed her guide. The worst, she wrote, was "crossing deep pits on rails which were so far apart I felt sure I could fall between them if I slipped." In Ajo, a village near the Mexican border, she climbed up a three-story-high tank full of acid to investigate reports that the fumes were worse at night. Feeling her way in the dark, she walked on a narrow path around the edge of the tank. "There was only a hand rail between me and that evil-looking, dark, bubbling acid," she wrote, "and I had the feeling all the time that if I stumbled I could so easily slip under the rail and plunge into the acid."

Much to her annoyance, Hamilton discovered that mining officials had hired spies to follow her. She asked the manager of one company why. "We think it wise," he replied, "to know as much as we can about people who come to this state on errands like yours." Years later, a retired mining engineer told her, "We thought you might be a troublemaker, but in the end we found you were perfectly impartial and fair."

"It Seemed Incredible at the Time"

In 1919, Harvard University—"the stronghold of masculinity against the inroads of women"—appointed Alice Hamilton an assistant professor of industrial medicine, the first woman professor. (In 1945, Harvard finally admitted women to its medical school.) "It seemed incredible at the time," Hamilton wrote, "but later on I came to understand it. . . . I was really about the only candidate available." That she was, for no women and few men in the world knew as much as she did about industrial poisons, especially lead. Nevertheless she had to agree to the following conditions: relinquish her right to use the Harvard Club and forgo her faculty allotment of football tickets. She also agreed not to march in the commencement procession or sit on the platform, even though, Hamilton noted, "each year I received a printed invitation to do so. At the bottom of the page would be the warning that 'under no circumstances may a woman sit on the platform.'"

Hamilton taught at Harvard until 1935, while continuing her investigations of poisonous substances, including aniline dye, benzene, and carbon disulphide. She wrote many articles and several books, including the first American textbook on industrial poisons.

In 1938, she conducted her last investigation. It was of the new viscose rayon industry. Hamilton documented the effects of several poisons used in the industry, including carbon disulphide. "There are few industrial diseases," she wrote, "which move one's sympathy more than does carbon disulphide poisoning. The first two cases I saw, one of slowly developing paralysis of the legs, the other of rapidly developing manic-depressive insanity, made a deep impression on me."

Her investigation revealed two familiar patterns: the reappearance of a poison in a new industry (carbon disulphide was once used in the rubber industry) and many reports about a particular poison in foreign medical journals but nothing in American journals. She also encountered the familiar problem of workers who were reluctant to be examined because they feared they would be fired.

"The story of this investigation . . . is not a pretty history," she wrote. The outcome, however, was positive. Hamilton's study conclusively proved to Americans that carbon disulphide was a poison. "The control of this dangerous trade," she wrote, "was slow in coming but when it came it was astonishingly rapid and complete."

For several years, an editor, who was also a cousin, had been urging Hamilton to write her autobiography. When she finally sent him a draft in 1942, he complained that "half the doors to you—the real Alice Hamilton are locked throughout,—your likes and dislikes, the exhilarations and disappointments you suffered in your work, the grief, the humor, and the love of people." In response, Hamilton reminded him that she was over seventy years old and not about to "become frank and outspoken and able to confide personal intimacies to the public," although she did respond to some of his suggestions. Her book, *Exploring the Dangerous Trades*, appeared in 1943 and received excellent reviews from critics, colleagues, strangers, and friends. "My God, how you and your sister Edith [a famous author of influential books about classical civilization, including *The Greek Way* and *The Roman Way*] can write," wrote one person.

Alice Hamilton lived to be an "old-old" woman. She shared a house built on the east bank of the Connecticut River in Hadlyme, Connecticut, with her sister Margaret and their close friend Clara Landsberg. Hamilton served as a consultant, gave lectures, and was active in the great liberal causes of her day. She was in her late eighties when her close friend Felix Frankfurter, a Supreme Court justice with whom she did not hesitate to disagree, observed that Hamilton was "a little more fragilely exquisite" but resolute in "her pugnacity of views regarding the things of which she disapproves." In particular, she disapproved of any limits on freedom of speech or association.

Hamilton welcomed each year that she lived. "We Hamiltons are a tough and long-lived lot," she explained after she recovered quickly from a broken hip. "Life is still as interesting as ever," she wrote when she was eighty-eight. "I should hate to leave it and not know what will happen next. Maybe we can sit on a cloud and watch."

She never had much money, but she was rich with family and friends and activities. She loved to cook (although she sometimes burned the pots), work in her garden, stay informed about national and world events, and write letters and articles. In her article "A Woman of Ninety Looks at Her World" Hamilton wrote, "Perhaps it is worthwhile for an old woman, much of whose life was spent among the submerged working

Alice Hamilton at age ninety.

class, to tell what life was really like underneath the pleasant, comfortable Victorian surface."

Alice Hamilton received many awards and honors but remained humble, even self-deprecating. "You see," she once wrote, "I simply cannot believe that I am a person of more than ordinary ability, though I know that chance has given me a more than ordinarily interesting life." When the president of Connecticut College informed her of the plan to name a dormitory after her and her sister Edith, Hamilton was pleased, but she insisted on one condition: "Edith's name must come first. It is not only that her writings on Greece and Rome will always be of lasting value, while mine on dangerous trades are already out-moded, but she is the elder sister, her name belongs in the first place."

Fifteen months after her sister Margaret died at the age of ninety-eight, Alice Hamilton died on September 22, 1970. She was 101 years old. "For me," she once wrote, "the satisfaction is that things are better now, and I had some part of it."

CHAPTER FIVE

"I Will Build Them Again"

MARY MCLEOD BETHUNE:
PASSIONATE EDUCATOR

1875–1955

MARY MCLEOD BETHUNE had a dream—"full equality for the Negro"—and she believed that education was the key. She had her dream during a time in America when it was nearly impossible, and often dangerous, for a black child to get an education, especially in southern states. Black children were not allowed in schools with white children, and there were very few separate schools for black children.

But Mary fought to make her dream come true, perhaps because she knew the story about how she was born with her eyes wide open. That meant, according to the midwife who delivered her, that Mary would always see things before they happened.

Mary was born in Sumter County, near Mayesville, South Carolina, a small town in a rice- and cotton-growing region. She was the fifteenth of seventeen children. Her parents, Patsy and Samuel McLeod, had been slaves. Like some other slaves

Mary McLeod Bethune's sisters Rachel and Maria were photographed standing in front of the cabin where Mary McLeod Bethune was born.

who were freed after the Civil War, Patsy McLeod continued to work for her former master, but now he had to pay her. Samuel McLeod did farmwork. They saved Patsy's wages until they had enough money to buy five acres of land from her former master. On that land, under a tall oak tree, the McLeods built their own small cabin, which they called the Homestead. Mary Jane was their first child to be born in the Homestead. And she was their first child to be born a free person.

Everyone in Mary's family worked hard to survive. Their day started at 5 A.M. After hitching up their mule, Old Bush, to the plow, everyone walked barefoot to the cotton field. Depending on the time of year, the McLeods plowed, spread fertilizer, planted cotton seeds, weeded, and picked cotton. When she was five years old, Mary's job was to sit on Old Bush, who got his name because of his bushy tail, and make sure that he pulled the plow in a straight line. By the time she was nine years old, Mary could pick 250 pounds (113 kg) of cotton a day. "I was my father's champion cotton picker," Bethune would later recall.

After eating supper and doing their evening chores, the McLeod family sat by the fireplace. They sang hymns and said their evening prayers. Mary's grandmother, Granny Sophia, sat in her rocker smoking a long-stemmed pipe. She had been a slave all her life, except as an old woman. Now her teeth were gone, and her skin was wrinkled. She always wore a red bandanna around her head. Her mother had been raised in a village in Africa before she was captured and brought to America on a slave ship. Granny Sophia told the stories about life in Africa that her mother told her. "The drums of Africa still beat in my heart," Mary once wrote when she herself was an old woman.

"Put Down That Book!"

Every week, Patsy McLeod earned money by washing and ironing clothes for her former slave master's family. Mary went with her when she delivered the clean clothes. One day, two little white girls, the former master's grandchildren, asked Mary to play with them. They showed her their toys and dolls and a new dollhouse. Then Mary picked up a book. She never forgot what happened next. One of the white girls yelled, "Put down that book! *You* can't read!"

It was true; Mary could not read. Neither could her mother, father, sisters, and brothers. Mary had no idea how she was going to learn to read. She just knew that she had to, so she hoped and prayed. She prayed often, especially while she was pulling weeds: "Please, God, help me get away from this crab grass. Help me to learn to read."

Then, one day, Emma Wilson knocked on the McLeods' door. That knock, Bethune wrote, "changed my life overnight. There stood a young woman, a colored missionary sent . . . to start a school nearby. She asked my parents to send me."

Mary was seven years old when she started Wilson's school. "Every morning I picked up a little pail of milk and bread, and walked five miles to school; every afternoon, five miles home. But I walked always on winged feet," she remembered. Mary learned to read. She learned writing, arithmetic, history, and geography. "As soon as I understood something, I rushed back and taught it to others at home," she said.

After four years in Wilson's school, Mary graduated. She wanted more education, but it was not possible. Old Bush had died, and her family had had to go into debt to buy another mule. For a year, Mary stayed at home doing chores and working in the cotton fields. "I used to kneel in the cotton fields and pray that the door of opportunity should be opened to me once more," she recalled.

Her prayers were answered when Mary Chrisman, a white teacher in Colorado, heard about Emma Wilson's school and offered to pay the tuition for one girl to continue her education. Wilson selected Mary. In the fall of 1887, Mary boarded a train to go to Scotia Seminary (now called Barber-Scotia College), a school for black girls in Concord, North Carolina.

At Scotia, Mary walked up her first stairway and slept on her first bed with sheets. She studied English, Latin, higher mathematics, and sciences, and she sang in the choir. She also worked in the laundry and kitchen to earn money for her room and board. During the summers, she babysat and cleaned houses. During her seven years at Scotia, Mary saved enough money to go home twice. She had both white and black teachers at Scotia. Mary always remembered how patient and kind they all were, and how they got along with each other. The teachers, she recalled, "taught that the color of a person's skin has nothing to do with his brains, and that color, caste, or class distinction are an evil thing."

After Mary McLeod graduated from Scotia, she wanted to go to Africa as a missionary, but church officials said no. First, they said, she had to study at the Bible Institute for Home and Foreign Missions in Chicago. There, McLeod studied the Bible and sang in the choir, often as the soloist. She also did mission work—visiting people in jails, feeding homeless people, and passing out religious leaflets. Out of a thousand students, Mary McLeod was the only black person. Years later, she wrote, "I have never been sensitive about my complexion. My color has never destroyed my self respect nor has it ever caused me to conduct myself in such a manner as to merit the disrespect of any person. . . . I would not exchange my color for all the wealth in the world, for had I been born white I might not have been able to do all that I have done or yet hope to do."

"*The Greatest Disappointment of My Life*"

After two years in Chicago, McLeod asked again to be sent to Africa. This time the church officials told her that there were no openings for black missionaries in Africa, just white missionaries. "The greatest disappointment of my life. Those were cruel days," she later wrote.

McLeod returned to Mayesville to teach with Emma Wilson. After a year, she went to teach eighth grade at the Haines Institute in Augusta, Georgia. Lucy Craft Laney, a former slave, was the founder and head of the Haines Institute. Laney rejected the common idea at the time that black children were inferior to white children, that black children could only grow up to do menial jobs. Her determination to prepare black children for better lives inspired many people, including Mary McLeod: "From her I got a new vision: my life work lay not in Africa but in my own country."

The next year, Mary McLeod went to Sumter, South Carolina, where she taught at the Kindell Institute. While singing in a church choir, she met Albertus Bethune. She had a beautiful voice, and so did he. Albertus taught Mary how to ride a bicycle, and they went on many rides together.

Mary and Albertus got married. A year later, their son was born, and she quit teaching to take care of him. Before long, Mary McLeod Bethune "got restless again to be back at my beloved work, for having a child made me more than ever determined to build better lives for my people." When she was asked to be in charge of a new school in Palatka, Florida, she accepted.

Bethune worked hard in her new job, and she started making plans to open her own school. "Whenever I accumulated a bit of money," she wrote, "I was off on an exploring trip, seeking a location where a new school would do the greatest good for the greatest number."

She finally settled on Daytona Beach, Florida, "a beautiful little village, shaded by great oaks and giant pines." Hundreds of black families were moving there to get jobs building the new Florida East Coast Railroad. Like all the towns Bethune visited, Daytona Beach had a white section and a black section. The white section had running water, paved roads, and many fine houses, including mansions. But the city had not provided running water or paved streets in the black section, known as "Colored Town." The only available houses were dilapidated shacks.

"Charred Splinters as Pencils"

On October 3, 1904, Mary McLeod Bethune opened her school. She called it the Daytona Educational and Industrial School for Negro Girls, and, at first, there were more words in

Mary McLeod Bethune with a line of girls from her school in about 1905.

its name than students (five young girls and her son, Albert). But she was confident that more students would come.

Bethune started her school with a promise and a dollar and a half. "I found a shabby four-room cottage, for which the owner wanted a rental of eleven dollars a month. My total capital was a dollar and a half, but I talked him into trusting me until the end of the month for the rest," she wrote. For a month, Bethune raised money. She rang doorbells, handed out leaflets, went to churches, clubs, lodges, and businesses. She rode her old bicycle over miles of dusty roads. "If a prospect refused to make a contribution I would say, 'Thank you for your time.' I refused to be discouraged," she wrote.

She raised just enough to pay the first month's rent. On the day that she opened her school, Bethune "hadn't a penny left." But that did not stop her. She was determined that her school would survive. "We burned logs and used the charred splinters as pencils, and mashed elderberries for ink. I begged strangers for a broom, a lamp. . . . I haunted the city dump and the trash piles behind hotels, retrieving discarded linen and kitchenware, cracked dishes, broken chairs, pieces of old lumber," Bethune later recalled.

Within a year, there were one hundred students and three assistant teachers. In two years, there were two hundred fifty students, more teachers, volunteers, and another building that Bethune used for classrooms and a dormitory. "As parents began gradually to leave their children overnight, I had to provide sleeping accommodations. I took corn sacks for mattresses. Then I picked Spanish moss from trees, dried and cured it, and used it as a substitute for mattress hair," she explained.

Many people pitched in to provide food, supplies, and money. Fishermen shared some of the fish they caught. Fruit growers donated bruised oranges that could not be sold. Railroad workers bought the sweet-potato pies that Bethune cooked and sold along the railroad tracks. Bethune solicited money from white people who came from the North to spend the winter in Florida. She also received money from many black people, including Madam C. J. Walker, president of the Madam C. J. Walker Manufacturing Company, who had built a business empire.

"Small Change Wrapped in My Handkerchief"

Every Sunday afternoon, Bethune held an open house. After she gave a short talk on black history, she and Albertus and other good singers would perform folk songs and spirituals. Before long, white visitors came to listen. "Strongly interracial" in her ideas, Bethune welcomed the white people. Soon, large crowds gathered for the open house.

Within two years, Bethune had "prayed up, sung up, and talked up" the first permanent building for her school. Four stories high with an open porch across the second-floor level, the building was called Faith Hall. It was built on a garbage dump that had been known as "Hell's Hole." The owner could not believe that Bethune wanted to buy a dump heap. But she did. He agreed to sell it for $250. She talked him into accepting five dollars down with the rest to be paid within two years. She raised the five dollars in a few days by selling ice cream and sweet-potato pies. "I took the owner his money in small change wrapped in my handkerchief," she wrote.

Mary McLeod Bethune did not stop at founding a school. After one of her students had an emergency operation at the hospital, Bethune found her segregated from the white patients in a corner of the porch behind the hospital kitchen. "Even my toes clenched with rage. That decided me. I called on three of my faithful friends, asking them to buy a little cottage behind our school as a hospital. They agreed, and we started with two beds." Before long, the two beds became a fully equipped twenty-bed hospital. Bethune named it McLeod Hospital, in honor of her parents.

In 1924, Bethune became president of the National Association of Colored Women, the highest office open to a black woman at that time. Later, she founded the National Council of Negro Women, a powerful organization that united more than eight hundred thousand black women to fight for civil rights. Bethune believed that "no race can stay down whose women rise."

In 1920, after a long and hard fight, black and white women had won the right to vote when the Nineteenth Amendment was ratified, or approved, by enough states to be added to the U.S. Constitution. But black people were discouraged from voting, especially in the South. Nevertheless, Bethune urged black people to vote. Her outspoken stand infuriated many white people in Daytona Beach, including the Ku Klux Klan, a secret organization that terrorized black people.

"If You Burn My Buildings"

Bethune was out of town the first time the Ku Klux Klan came to her school to threaten her. But she was there the second time they came. It was the night before election day. Hiding under white hoods and robes, about eighty men rode to the school carrying lighted torches and a large cross that they stuck in the ground and set on fire. The Klan's friends in the city had turned off all the streetlights. But Bethune's school had a generator to make its own electricity, and she ordered every light inside and outside the school turned on. In the blaze of her own lights, Bethune faced down the Klansmen.

"If you burn my buildings, I'll build them again. And if you burn them a second time, I'll build them again!" she said. Then Bethune and her students began to sing, "Be not dismayed what e'er betide, God will take care of us!" Silently the Ku Klux Klan left.

Bethune went to vote the next morning. She and other black voters were forced to wait all day. But they waited and voted, and the Klan's candidate was defeated.

People throughout America wanted to meet Mary McLeod Bethune. She gave countless speeches. And she sang. "Oh, how she could sing! It was a joy to hear her and an inspiration to touch her glowing life," wrote one of Bethune's many friends. She traveled to Europe and met the Pope in Rome and the lord mayor of London. In Scotland she dined with a distant relative of her parents' former slave master. In Paris she met with a group of African scholars. In Switzerland she climbed mountains. Back in the United States, President Calvin Coolidge asked her for advice. So did President Herbert Hoover, who appointed her to government commissions on child welfare and home building and ownership. Then, during a terrible time in America, President Franklin Delano Roosevelt asked for her help.

Roosevelt had been elected president in 1932, when the United States was in a dreadful crisis—the Great Depression. Millions of people had lost their jobs and their homes. Long lines of men and women and children waited for hours to get free food at soup kitchens. Determined to end the crisis, Roosevelt introduced many new programs, which he called the New Deal. To help young people, Roosevelt created the National Youth Administration (NYA). At first Roosevelt asked Bethune to be an adviser to the NYA. But, in 1936, he appointed her director of the NYA Division of Negro Affairs. "The NYA," Bethune wrote, "is building a new emancipation for Negro youth from the despair of denied opportunity."

Bethune was a fierce advocate for civil rights. She carried signs and picketed businesses in Washington, D.C., that refused to hire black people. She spoke at rallies. She defied segregation by refusing to sit in separate sections or ride in freight elevators or enter through back doors. "Prejudice of all kinds must be forgotten and we must concern ourselves with universal peace, universal education, and universal religion," she said.

When the United States entered World War II in 1941, Bethune became a special assistant to the secretary of war. She helped select black women for the Women's Army Corps (WAC). Like all the armed forces, the WAC was segregated, an accepted way of life in America. Bethune worked hard to get the fairest treatment possible for black women in the military. When the war ended, she was one of fifty delegates from the United States invited to help write the charter for the United Nations.

In 1949, Mary McLeod Bethune left Washington, D.C., and

Mary McLeod Bethune in her office. Behind her are photographs of famous people whom she worked with in various ways, including Madam C. J. Walker, a successful businesswoman, pictured in the oval frame and Franklin Delano Roosevelt, president of the United States from 1933 to 1945, pictured in the largest square frame.

returned to her cottage, the Retreat, on the campus of her school—which had grown into a college, Bethune-Cookman College. She enjoyed the company of students, friends, and her son, Albert, and his family. Many years earlier, she and Albertus had separated.

By this time, she was a living legend. People made pilgrimages to talk with her. A popular magazine, *Ebony*, published an article that she titled "My Last Will and Testament."

"Sometimes as I sit communing in my study," she wrote, "I feel that death is not far off. I am aware that it will overtake me before the greatest of my dreams—full equality for the Negro in our time—is realized." She went on to list nine "principles and policies" that she believed represented the meaning of her life's work. She hoped that her philosophy would give people everywhere inspiration:

I leave you love. . . . I leave you hope. . . . I leave you the challenge of developing confidence in one another. . . . I leave you a thirst for education. . . . I

Mary McLeod Bethune loved to collect walking sticks and is portrayed on this statue holding one in her right hand. A copy of her last will is in her left hand. Statues of a boy and a girl are portrayed with open arms and hands, as if to receive her last will.

leave you a respect for the uses of power. . . . I leave you faith. . . . I leave you racial dignity. . . . I leave you a desire to live harmoniously with your fellow men. . . . I leave you finally a responsibility to our young people.

Mary McLeod Bethune received many awards and honors for her work, including the Medal of Honor and Merit from the government of Haiti. She died in 1955 and was buried on the campus of Bethune-Cookman College.

"Whirlwind of Work"

KATHARINE WORMELEY:
DARING SUPERINTENDENT

1830–1908

KATHARINE WORMELEY did not see the Union soldiers fighting during the Battle of Seven Pines. She just heard the cannons booming. But she knew that the battle would leave her with "a whirlwind of work, sad work." She knew that because she was a "superintendent of nursing" on board a hospital transport ship anchored in the York River near the site of the battle.

Several days after the battle, Wormeley wrote a letter to her sister Ariana and described the aftermath: "Men in every condition of horror, shattered and shrieking, were being brought in on stretchers. The men had mostly been without food for three days. . . . We began to do what we could. . . . Fortunately we had plenty of lemons, ice, and . . . a barrel of molasses, which with vinegar, ice, and water, made a most refreshing drink. After that we gave them crackers and milk, or tea and bread. Imagine a great river steamer filled on every deck, every berth and every square inch of room covered with wounded men;

even the stairs and gangways filled with those who are less badly wounded."

The Battle of Seven Pines, also known as the Battle of Fair Oaks, was one of many battles that took place during the Civil War. The fighting began in 1861, when northern states (known as the Union) and southern states (known as the Confederacy) went to war over the issue of slavery. Katharine Wormeley hated slavery, and she was determined to help the Union. However, at that time in history women of her class were expected to devote themselves to their homes and families. But Wormeley was determined to help fight the war. She had grown up hearing about how her grandfather, a member of a prominent family in Virginia, had freed his family's slaves. He had also moved his family to England to make sure that his son (Katharine's father) would not become a slaveholder. Throughout her life, Wormeley was inspired by her grandfather and father. She described her father as having a "passionate love of freedom and hatred of oppression."

Katharine Wormeley was born in England on January 14, 1830. Her family encouraged her to develop her mind, and she studied in England, France, and Switzerland. When the Civil War began, she was living in Newport, Rhode Island. Without hesitation, Wormeley set about finding useful work to do. She founded a Women's Union Aid Society and organized women to make bandages, blankets, and raise money. She also helped soldiers' wives and daughters by starting a factory where they could earn money by making shirts for the government. During

Katharine Wormeley.

the first winter of the war, the women produced some fifty thousand shirts.

On May 7, 1862, Wormeley received a telegram informing her that the *Daniel Webster*, a hospital ship from the Hospital Transport Service, had arrived in New York City with the first load of sick and wounded soldiers from the Peninsula Campaign in Virginia. In a letter to her sister Ariana, Wormeley wrote, "If I wish to join the Hospital Transport Service, I must be in New York tomorrow morning. So I leave tonight." Several days later, the *Daniel Webster* with Wormeley on board arrived in Virginia to help sick and wounded soldiers.

The Peninsula Campaign was led by Union General George B. McClellan. It started in March 1862, when McClellan had a huge army transported by ships to the tip of the Virginia peninsula that lies between the York and James rivers. From there, McClellan planned to move his huge army seventy miles up the peninsula and capture Richmond, Virginia, the Confederate capital. However, McClellan's plans did not include caring for the sick and wounded soldiers. At the time of the Civil War, the common belief was that military personnel and equipment should not be burdened by the needs of sick and wounded soldiers, especially under difficult conditions. And the low, swampy, mosquito-infested peninsula was definitely a difficult place. Unless someone offered to help the military authorities, sick and wounded soldiers would have to fend for themselves.

"Efficient, Wise, Active as Cats"

Fortunately, help was offered by a group of citizens who had formed the United States Sanitary Commission to provide soldiers with medicine, clothing, food, and supplies. For the Peninsula Campaign, the Sanitary Commission proposed a bold plan. Since the fighting would take place on swampy land near major rivers, the plan was to convert ships into floating hospitals to save sick and wounded soldiers and transport them to regular hospitals in Philadelphia, New York City, Boston, and Washington, D.C.

Frederick Law Olmsted, head of the Sanitary Commission, presented the plan to the military authorities. All the authorities had to do was provide ships and the Sanitary Commission would turn the ship into a hospital ship. Olmsted and his workers would scrub, deodorize, repair, rebuild, supply, and run the floating hospitals. The authorities agreed, and the Hospital Transport Service was established.

The *Daniel Webster* was the first ship to be converted. Before long, the Hospital Transport Service had a launch that could go up small rivers, barges, a contraption that ran up and down railroad tracks, and six ships, including the *Wilson Small*, the headquarters for the Hospital Transport Service. Olmsted was the overall director, and Katharine Wormeley was one of four "superintendents of nursing." In a letter to a friend, Wormeley described Olmsted: "He is small and lame . . . but though the lameness is decided, it is scarcely observable, for he gives you a sense that he triumphs over it by doing as if it did not exist. . . .

The U.S. Sanitary Commission Steamer Daniel Webster.

He has great variety of expression: sometimes stern, thought-ful, and haggard; at other times observing and slightly satirical (I believe he sees out of the back of his head occasionally)." As for the other superintendents—Christine Griffin, Georgeanna "Georgy" Woolsey, and Eliza Howland—Wormeley described them as "efficient, wise, active as cats, merry, [and] light-hearted."

The superintendents had little time to rest. In addition to supervising the nurses, who were all men, they were in charge of supplies, housekeeping, cooking, and caring for patients. They also went on patrols through the swamps looking for sick and wounded soldiers. In a letter to Ariana, Wormeley described how she and Georgy managed to get some rest: "I have learned to sleep on my arm, and it is very 'comfy.' As for Georgy, she curls herself up anywhere, like a little gray kitten, and is asleep in a minute." Wormeley also told Ariana how they dealt with dirt and stains:

> My dresses are in such a state that I loathe them, and myself in them. From chin to belt they are yellow with lemon-juice, sticky with sugar, greasy with beef-tea, and pasted with mild-porridge. "Georgy," I said the other day, "What am I to do? I can't put on that dress again, and the other is a great deal worse."
>
> "I know what I shall do. Dr. Agnew had some flannel shirts; he is going back to New York, and can't want them. I shall get him to give me one," says Georgy, who is never at a loss, and suggests the wildest things in the calmest way. Accordingly, Santa Georgeanna has appeared in an easy and graceful costume. I took the hint, and have followed suit in a flannel shirt from the hospital supplies.

As McClellan moved his huge army up the peninsula toward Richmond, the hospital ships followed along on the James River. Sick and wounded soldiers arrived at all times of the day and night. In a letter to her mother Wormeley wrote, "We are awakened in the dead of night by a sharp steam-whistle, and soon after feel ourselves clawed by little tugs on either side of our big ship, bringing off the sick and wounded from the shore. And, at once, the process of taking on hundreds of men—many of them crazed with fever—begins." Wormeley also wrote about making excursions to rescue soldiers. On one occasion, she and some others went out late at night in a thunderstorm and rescued fifty-six men. According to Wormeley, "The return passage was rather an anxious one. The river was much obstructed with sunken ships and trees; the night was dark, and we had to feel our way, slackening speed every ten minutes."

On another occasion, a hospital boat with two hundred men aboard ran aground at night. In a letter to her mother, Wormeley wrote, "Of course they had to be attended to. So, amidst the wildest and most beautiful storm of thunder and lightning, four of us pulled off to her in a little boat, with tea, bread, brandy, and beef-essence. No one can tell how it tries my nerves to go toppling round at night in little boats, and clambering up ships' sides on little ladders."

Many of the sick and wounded men asked Wormeley to write letters for them. "Such letters are often very funny. Some few told the horror of the march; but as a rule they were all about the families at home," she wrote to Ariana.

The Union army got within eight miles of Richmond. But that was it. After a series of battles, McClellan decided to pull back, a move that some people called the "great skedaddle." McClellan's plan had failed. However, Katharine Wormeley and the members of the Hospital Transport Service had not failed. They had rescued almost ten thousand soldiers. Because of their work, military authorities finally realized that it was possible to save sick and wounded soldiers even when they were fighting in difficult places. So, the military authorities agreed to run the Hospital Transport Service themselves. After

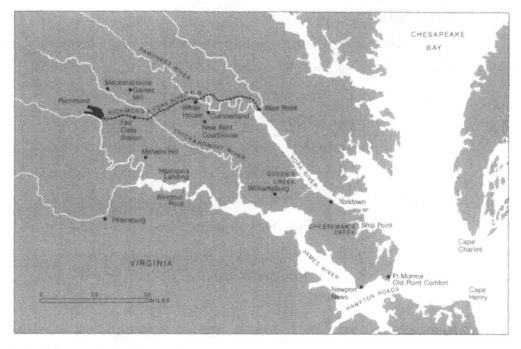

Map of Virginia Peninsula, 1862.

---

three months of service, Katharine Wormeley and the rest of the Sanitary Commission workers could leave the Virginia Peninsula.

On July 25, 1862, Wormeley wrote in a letter, "Georgy and Mr. Olmsted and I sat up the greater part of our last night on the *Webster*, talking. . . . It is sad to feel that it is all over. The last I saw of Mr. Olmsted he was disappearing over the side of the *Webster*, clad in the garb of a fashionable gentleman. I rubbed my eyes, and felt that it was indeed all over. I myself had risen to the occasion by putting on a black lace tablespoon [bonnet] in which I became at once conventional and duly civilized."

Katharine Wormeley returned to Newport exhausted.

Nevertheless, within a month she had agreed to become a superintendent, or head, of a military hospital near Newport. Georgy Woolsey and her sister Jane came to work with Wormeley as assistant superintendents. In a letter to her mother, Jane wrote, "Miss Wormeley, our chief, is clever, spirited and energetic in the highest degree—a cultivated woman, with friends and correspondents among the best literary men here and in England, . . . a great capacity for business and not a single grain of mock-sentiment about her."

"Shoulder to Shoulder"

After the Civil War ended in 1865, Katharine Wormeley continued her whirlwind of work. She trained poor women for jobs and founded an industrial school for girls. She was renowned for her work in translating French novels into English, in particular the books of Honoré de Balzac.

Wormeley maintained an ardent correspondence with Frederick Law Olmsted. They wrote letters about what they were reading, where they were traveling, and what they were doing. They discussed ideas and politics, often expressing strong differences. Their correspondence mysteriously ended after seventeen years, and Wormeley destroyed Olmsted's letters to her. Fourteen years later, they resumed writing letters to each other, although without the intensity, until Olmsted's death ten years later.

When she heard of his death, Wormeley wrote a letter to her friend Emma Brace and recalled Olmsted's words to her:

"Remember, whatever comes in life, nothing can ever make me lose my perfect confidence in you." As for her sentiments, she wrote to Emma that Olmsted was one of the "men I had loved best in life."

In 1888, twenty-seven years after the Civil War, Katharine Wormeley published a book with letters she wrote when she was a superintendent on board the hospital transport ship titled *The Other Side of War.* She published the letters exactly as she had written them. In one letter she described the three months on the ships as "a period to look back upon when we worked together under the deepest feelings, and to the extent of our powers, shoulder to shoulder, helping each other to the best of our ability, no one failing or hindering another."

Katharine Wormeley died in Jackson, New Hampshire, in 1908.

LETTER EXCERPTS FROM
THE OTHER SIDE OF WAR

During her three months as a superintendent of nursing, Katharine Wormeley wrote letters to her mother, her sister Ariana (whom she addresses as "A."), and to friends whom she does not name. Each letter has the date and the name of the ship Wormeley was on when she wrote the letter. Some letters were written on shore, where Wormeley waited for trains that carried sick and wounded soldiers from the battlefields.

U.S. FLOATING HOSPITAL *DANIEL WEBSTER*

OFF SHIP POINT, MAY 10 [1862]

Dear Friend,

I write with a pencil, because it is so comfortable. We left New York yesterday at 5 P.M. . . . We stayed on deck by moonlight till eleven o'clock, when I turned in, to sleep all night, and get up lazily to breakfast at nine this morning. Since then I have helped to make our hospital-flag, and have dreamed away the day, lying on deck in the sweet air, where I could see the bluest sky and the bluest water (when the vessel dipped) and nothing else.

———————

HEADQUARTERS U.S. SANITARY COMMISSION, STEAMER *WILSON SMALL*
OFF YORKTOWN, MAY 12

Dear A.,

Transferred to this boat. Mr. Olmsted came on board at twelve o'clock last night and ordered Mrs. Griffin and me off the *Daniel Webster.* We had just received, stowed, and fed two hundred and forty-five men, most of them very ill with typhoid fever. The ship sailed at eight o'clock this morning, and will be in New York tomorrow night [where the patients were transferred to a hospital and then the ship returned for more patients]. . . . The men were all patient and grateful. Some said, "You don't know what it is to me to see you. This is heaven, after what I've suffered. To think a woman being here to help me!" . . . One little drummer-boy thought he was going to die instantly. I said: "Pooh! You'll walk off the ship in New York. Take your tea."

———————

WILSON SMALL, MAY 13

Dear Mother,

Yours [letter] of the ninth received. The mails come with sufficient regularity. We all rush at the letter-bags, and think ourselves blighted beings if we get nothing. Yesterday I came on board this boat, where there are thirty very bad cases—four or five amputations. One poor fellow, a lieutenant in the

Thirty-second New York Volunteers, shot through the knee, and enduring more than mortal agony; a fair haired boy of seventeen, shot through the lungs, every breath he draws hissing through the wound; another man, a poet, with seven holes in him, but irrepressibly poetic and very comical. He dictated to me last night a foolscap sheet full of poetry composed for the occasion. His appearance as he sits up in bed, swathed in a nondescript garment or poncho, constructed for him by Miss Whetten out of an old green table-cloth, is irresistibly funny.

———+———

WILSON SMALL, MAY 14

Dear Mother,

We are now making ready to run up the Pamunky River as far as the advance of the army at Cumberland, this boat, the *Wilson Small*, is disabled. She was twice run into today,—the second time by the huge *Vanderbilt*, which nearly demolished her. We are to be towed by the *Knickerbocker* as far as West Point, where there is a shipyard. You must get a map and follow us—or rather the army and us. . . . The general opinion is that a fearful struggle will take place before Richmond. Alas! But it is not a battle which destroys so many lives as it is the terrible decimating diseases brought on by exposure and hardships and the climate or marshes and watercourses. The majority of the cases of illness which I have seen were men who dropped exhausted from the army on its march, and had painfully made their way to the banks of creeks and rivers, where they were picked up by passing boats and brought down to us.

WILSON SMALL, MAY 16

Dear Friend,

We all know in our hearts that it is thorough enjoyment to be here,—*it is life*, in short; and we wouldn't be anywhere else for anything in the world. I hope people will continue to sustain the Sanitary Commission. Hundreds of lives are being saved by it. I have seen with my own eyes in one week fifty men who must have died without it, and many more who probably would have done so.

S. R. SPAULDING, PAMUNKY RIVER

MAY 17

Dear Mother,

After dinner we ran up to West Point, where the York River fords, the northern branch being the Mattapony (pronounced Mattapo*ni*); the other the Pamunky, along the line of which the army has advanced. . . . They have had the pluck to run this huge vessel up this little river, without a chart, and not a soul on board who has been here before. The passage has been enchanting; we ran so close to the shore that I could almost have thrown my glove upon it. The verdure is in its freshest spring beauty; the lovely shores are filled with trees and shrubs of every brilliant and tender shade of green, broken now and then by creeks, running up little valleys till they are lost in the blue distance. I saw the beginning of the battlefield of Williamsburg, . . . and the whole of the battlefield of West Point, still dotted with the hospital tents, from which we have cleared out all the wounded.

———+———

SPAULDING, MAY 20

Dear Mother,

The weather is delightful. At present we are idle, kept so, I am told, in reserve for the expected battle. The *Elm City* is to remain here as a receiving ship; this vessel (the *Spaulding*) and the *Daniel Webster* are to be used as ocean transports, and chiefly for sick men; the *Knickerbocker* and the *Daniel Webster No. 2* as river transports for wounded men,—"surgical cases," as they are called. The former make the sea-passages to New York, Boston, or Philadelphia; the latter run to Washington or Fortress Monroe. These five ships can transport about two thousand men a week.

———+———

SPAULDING, MAY 23

Dear A.,

We go on board some newly arrived ships, and find the parties in charge of the invoices: sixteen pail! we'll take eight; . . .

"Essences of beef! we want all of that," "What fifty cans? Fifty! we must have hundred,"—and so on through sugar, arrowroot, farina, spices, lemons, whiskey, brandy, etc,. . . . Kleptomania is the prevailing disease among us. . . . After such a visit, Georgy's unfathomable pocket is a mine of wealth as to nutmeg-graters, corkscrews, forks and spoons and such articles. . . . I, being less nimble at pilfering, content myself by carrying off tin pails with an abstract air. Perhaps our visits do not give the keen satisfaction to others that they do to us. But *they* are going back where they can get more; while to us who remain here, such articles are as precious as if they were made of gold.

KNICKERBOCKER, MAY 26

Dear Mother,
It is a piteous sight to see these men; no one knows what war is until they see this black side of it. We may all sentimentalize over its possibilities as we see the regiments go off, or when we hear of a battle; but it is as far from the reality as to read of pain is far from feeling it.

KNICKERBOCKER, MAY 31

Dear Mother,
The long letter now enclosed I was too utterly tired out to carry even the length of the ward to post last night. As I finished it,

two steamers came alongside, each with a hundred sick on board, bringing word that the *Louisiana* (a side-wheel vessel, not a commission boat) was aground a little distance, with two hundred more, having no one in charge of them and nothing to eat. Of course, they had to be attended to. So, amid the wildest and most beautiful storm of thunder and lightning, Georgy, Dr. Ware, Mrs. Reading, and I pulled off to her in a little boat with tea, bread, brandy, and beef-essence. . . . We fed them,—the usual process,—poor fellows, they were so crazy. . . . All the time the thunder was incessant, the rain falling in torrents, while every second the beautiful crimson lightning flashed the whole scene open to us. . . . Do you wonder, therefore, that I forgot to mail your letter?

———————+———————

WILSON SMALL, JUNE 1

Dear A.,

I write amid the distant booming of cannon and the hourly arrival of telegrams from the scene of action. The battle (Seven Pines) began yesterday afternoon. Up to 11 P.M. the accounts received were not wholly favorable. The attack was made on our weakest point, General Casey's division, which is the advanced body on the Chickahominy. It was attacked on front and flank, and retreated; but being reinforced by General Heintzelman, the ground and a lost battery were recovered. The second telegram to Colonel Ingalls was written off by the operator on the envelope of your letter of the 26th; I shall keep it as a souvenir. It says; "General Kearny has driven the enemy a mile at the point of the bayonet. General Heintzel- man is driving back the enemy. . . ." A little later, and we heard, "We are driving them before us at every point;" and now the last word is, "Our victory is complete." The wounded are pouring in. . . .

———◆———

WILSON SMALL, JUNE 2

Dear A.,

What a whirlwind of work, sad work, we have been in! Immediately after closing my letter of yesterday, Mrs. Griffin and I were whisked away in a little boat, at the peril of our lives, and hustled, tumbled, hoisted, first into the *State of Maine*, where we lost our way amid frightful scenes, until we finally reached the *Elm City*, where we were going as night-watch to relieve the ladies belonging to her, who had been up all the night before. She had four hundred and seventy wounded men on board. . . . The surgeons let them, for the most part, have a night's rest before their wounds were opened. Not so, however, on the *State of Maine*, where operations were going on all night; the hideous sounds filling our ears. . . . The victory *is* a victory; but oh, the lives and the suffering it has cost!

Dear Mother,

We went on board [the *Vanderbilt*]; and such a scene as we entered and lived in for two days I trust never to see again. Men in every condition of horror, shattered and shrieking, were being brought in on stretchers. . . . We began to do what we could. The first thing wanted by wounded men is something to drink. . . . Fortunately we had plenty of lemons, ice, and sherry on board. . . . Dr. Ware discovered a barrel of molasses, which, with vinegar, ice, and water, made a most refreshing drink. . . . The horrors of that morning are too great to speak of. . . . I do not suffer under the sights; but, oh, the sounds, the screams of men. . . . Last night, shining over blood and agony, I saw a lunar rainbow; and in the afternoon a peculiarly beautiful effect of rainbow and stormy sunset,—it flashed upon my eyes as I passed an operating table, and raised them to avoid seeing anything as I passed.

Dear Friend,

This is the first quiet Sunday since we have been here. . . . I trust the worst is over. . . . I have seen many men die. . . . I hope you may be happy this summer, it would be something to be able to think of happiness as existing somewhere.

ON SHORE, JUNE 9

Dear Mother,

I can't retain the least recollection of when I write, or what I write, or to whom it is written. I only know that I do write to somebody nearly every day. . . . Sometimes the intense excitement of our lives finds vent and ease in writing. . . . We have so many letters to scribble for the poor fellows that materials must always be handy. I go about with my notepaper rolled up in a magazine and stuck, with pens and ink, into an apron-pocket. . . . Besides the letters we write and send off for the men, we have many from friends inquiring after husbands, sons and brothers who are reported wounded. . . . One came last week from a wife inquiring after her husband, . . . Mrs. Griffin remembered the name; he was one of the men whose funeral she attended ashore one Sunday evening. So to-day I went up and found him under the feathery elm-tree. I made a little sketch of the place and sent it to her,—all I could send, poor soul!

WILSON SMALL, JUNE 12

Dear A.,

I hope you keep my letters (for my own benefit). I have no recollection of where I have been or what I have done. You can form no idea of the bewilderment and doubt in which we live as to times and seasons, hours of the day and days of the week.

It is really absurd. I am told today is Thursday; but I certainly thought it was Tuesday.

Dear A.,

Yesterday we did nothing special but dress in clean clothes (I mean the cleanest we had) and go down to the *Webster*, where we were received with all honors, and had a *good* dinner. Georgy and I eating an incredible number of raspberry tartlets. Dr. Grymes drank to us in his happiest manner: "Ladies, I give you a *welcome!*" The ship was dressed with magnolia, honeysuckle, and the lovely white fringe blossoms in our honor.

Dear Mother,

A train arrives and . . . the wounded men are sent at once on board whichever transport lies at the wharf. The cars [railroad] are large, double freight cars. The worst cases lie upon the floor inside; the slight cases sit upon the roof. . . . We must either laugh or cry; and this work teaches us that we had better laugh, if we mean to be good for anything.

—————✦—————

Dear Mother,

I saw her [Georgy] today spring from the ground to the floor
of a freight car, with a can of beef tea in one hand, her flask in
the other, and a row of tin cups tied round her waist. Our
precious flasks! They do us good service at every turn. We
wear them slung over our shoulders by a bit of ribbon or an
end of rope. If, in the "long hereafter of song," some poet
should undertake to immortalize us, he'll do it thus, if he's an
honest man and sticks to truth:

> "A lady with a flask shall stand
> Beef tea and punch in either hand
> Heroic mass of mud
> And dirt and stains and blood."

—————✦—————

OFF BERKLEY, HARRISON'S BAR, JAMES RIVER,
TUESDAY, JULY 1, 1862

Dear Mother,

We arrived here [Harrison's Landing on the James River]
yesterday to hear the thunder of the battle [of Malvern Hill]
and to find the army just approaching this landing. Last night
it was a verdant shore; today it is a dusty plain. The feelings
with which we came up the James River I can't describe, our
anxiety, excitement, and breathless desire to know *something*
was so great. . . . We were just admiring a fine old colonial

house, when someone standing in the bow cried, "I see something white among the trees to the right!" and in a few minutes more we made them out to be army wagons. We had met our army! What next were we to learn? Never shall I forget the look of the first officers who came on board,—one a major, the other a chaplain. They were gaunt and haggard, their hair stood out from their heads stiffened with dust and dirt, their faces were nearly black, and to their waists they were literally moulded in Virginia clay. "Oh! what is this?" we cried. "Is it defeat?" "Defeat! No! We have retreated, but we never turned our backs on them. We have faced and fought and beaten them for five days!"

WILSON SMALL, HARRISON'S LANDING,
JULY 3

Dear A.,

I am sitting on deck. Poor Miss Lowell, whose gallant brother was killed yesterday, is beside me. She belongs to the *Daniel Webster*, which is to load up this afternoon. We are lying a stone's throw from a long wharf. . . . The long wharf is a moving mass of human beings: on one side, a stream of men unloading the commissariat and the other stores; on the other, a sad procession of wounded, feebly crawling . . . to go on board the transports. . . . *This is war*, and there's no more to be said about it.

WILSON SMALL, HARRISON'S LANDING,
MONDAY, JULY 7

Dear Mother,

The weather is intensely hot. My hand wets and sticks to the
paper as I write. The thermometer at the door of my stateroom
is 98°. We cannot put our faces out upon deck without
blistering them in the fierce glare of sun and water.

WILSON SMALL, JULY 8

Dear Mother,

For the last two hours, I have been watching President Lincoln
and General McClellan as they sat together, in earnest conver-
sation, on the deck of a steamer close to us. I am thankful, I am
happy, that the President has come . . . to see and hear and
judge for his own wise and noble self. . . . They sat together,
apparently with a map between them, to which McClellan
pointed from time to time with the end of his cigar . . . then
they rose and walked side by side ashore, the President, in a
shiny black coat and stovepipe hat, a whole head and shoulders taller, as it seemed to me, than the General.

Dear A.,

This morning I went ashore [to see the new government hospital for soldiers] without orders and, indeed, without permission. I was so anxious to see for myself the state of things that I could not forego the chance. The hospital occupies the Harrison House, and a barn, out-buildings, and several tents at the rear. We stayed about three hours with the men, writing letters for them. Such letters are often very funny. Some few told the horrors of the march; but as a rule they were all about the families at home. . . . I am glad I went ashore, for now I am quite content to go home. Our work—I mean the women's work—is over, except on the *Webster* and the *Spaulding*, which must still make two or three trips in the service of the Commission.

Dear Friend,

I have slept in my own bed! . . . The Hospital Transport Service is ended. Georgy and Mr. Olmsted and I sat up the greater part of our last night on the *Webster*, talking as people will who know that on the morrow they are to be separate widely. . . . This expedition . . . has made a body of life-long friends. . . . From first to last there has been perfect accord among us. . . . It is sad to feel that it is all over. . . . A short three months ago I wrote to tell you it was beginning; but what lifetime lies between then and now.

CHAPTER SEVEN

"For the Sum of Love and Affection and Ten Dollars"

BIDDY MASON: FIERCE FIGHTER

1818–1891

BIDDY MASON'S adventure started with a walk—about a two-thousand-mile walk from Mississippi to California, via Salt Lake City, Utah. At the time, she was a slave who worked in the cotton fields, tended to the animals, and used her knowledge of herbal medicine to heal sick people and her skills as a midwife to deliver babies.

But before I continue with Mason's adventure, let me tell you about how I first "met" her during a trip to California in 1995.

As was my custom, I had identified places where I could find women's history: markers, monuments, memorials, gravesites, houses, historic sites, museums, and archives. When I got to Los Angeles, I went in search of the Biddy Mason Memorial. I assumed from the address I had— "between Spring Street and Broadway at Third Street"—that I would see the memorial from the street. That was not the case. Back and forth I wandered. Finally I found someone who told me to go to the

The entrance to the Biddy Mason Memorial from the Bradbury Building is at the rear of the photograph. The X on the wall in the foreground is a replica of the mark Biddy Mason used to sign her name.

Bradbury Building on Broadway. There I entered an architectural jewel built in 1893 with a central atrium that extended five stories up to a huge skylight. As I gazed in amazement at the beautiful interior, a guard approached me.

"It's Saturday," he said. "All the offices are closed."

"I'm looking for the Biddy Mason Memorial," I replied.

"Out that back door," he said, pointing across the lobby.

Out that back door, I stepped into an exquisite, narrow, vest-pocket park created in a space surrounded by the Bradbury

Building, a new parking garage, and an arcade with small shops. To my right, I saw a long, black wall with ten gray granite panels.

Slowly, I walked beside the wall that I later discovered is eighty-one feet long and eight feet high. It is titled *Biddy Mason's Place: A Passage of Time* and was created by Sheila Levrant de Bretteville. Each of the ten panels represents a decade from 1810 to 1900. A series of dates and words are incised into each panel, with inserts of photographs, maps, and drawings on slate panels. There are two succinct narratives, one about the development of Los Angeles when "forty-four settlers from Mexico established the pueblo of Los Angeles—twenty-six have African ancestors."

The other narrative is about Biddy Mason. The text is in two font sizes designed by Bretteville. The larger-sized font outlines the highlights of her life:

Biddy Mason born a slave.

She learns midwifery.

She walks to California behind a wagon train.

She wins freedom in court.

She owns land.

She delivers hundreds of babies.

Los Angeles mourns and reveres Grandma Mason.

Words in the smaller font add more details:

Eighteen year old Biddy and her sister Hannah become the property of Robert Smith. . . .

Smith transports slaves to California, a free state, where Judge Hayes declares Biddy Mason's family entitled to freedom and free forever.

From ten years' wages Biddy saves $250 to buy this homestead lots 3 and 8, Block 7 of the Ord Survey, a bit out of town, amid gardens and groves.

Biddy nurses the sick, comforts prisoners, and pays a grocery store at 4th and Spring streets to feed all the families made homeless by seasonal floods.

The images include historic maps and views of Los Angeles, a picket fence, a large wagon wheel, a midwife's bag, a spool of thread, scissors, and the X that Mason used to sign her name, since she could neither read nor write. Photographs of her freedom papers and the deed to her property are bonded to pieces of limestone set into the wall. The final image on the last panel is the only known photograph of Biddy Mason, a full-face portrait of an unsmiling and resolute-looking woman.

Just beyond the wall, I found another memorial titled *Biddy Mason: House of the Open Hand*, by Betye Saar. It covers two walls in the elevator lobby of the parking garage. On one wall is a photomural of Mason and three other women sitting on the front porch of the Owens's, her friends and neighbors. The other wall is an assemblage with the "Window of Memories" that includes items historically associated with women—a fan,

a curled window shade, a medicine bottle, wallpaper, a cur-
tain—and Mason's photograph.

All this, of course, made me
curious to learn more about
Biddy Mason and about this
memorial. I searched for and
found newspaper articles, including "A Lot of History" by
Myrna Oliver; books, including
The Power of Place by Dolores
Hayden, who headed the effort
to build the memorial; and
articles posted on the Internet,

A close-up of the image of Biddy Mason on the wall.

including "Biddy Mason's Place: A Passage of Time" by Betye
Saar and Sheila Levrant de Bretteville. I also located and read
the *Autobiography of John Brown*, the leader of one of the wagon
trains that Mason walked behind. From these sources, I pieced
together her story.

"Born a Slave"

Biddy (she took the name Mason much later in life) was
born a slave, probably in Georgia. There are no accounts of
her growing-up years until she became the property of slave
owners in Mississippi, Robert and Rebecca Smith, when she
was eighteen years old. But, judging by the skills she had, she
grew up learning how to handle livestock and prepare and

administer herbal medicines and deliver babies. Mason herself later talked about how often she had to provide nursing care to Rebecca Smith.

Biddy Mason was thirty years old when Robert Smith decided to migrate with his family and slaves to the Utah Territory. A recent convert to the Church of Jesus Christ of Latter-day Saints, commonly called the Mormon Church, Smith wanted to join the newly established Mormon community in the Great Salt Lake Basin. In March 1848, he and his family joined a group of other Mormons in Fulton, Mississippi, in the northeast corner of the state near the Alabama border. There were nine white people in his party and ten slaves, including Mason, her three daughters—ten-year-old Ellen, four-year-old Ann, and baby Harriet who was still nursing—and her half-sister Hannah. Mason's job was to walk behind the ox-drawn wagons and herd the livestock. That, plus taking care of her children, and most likely tending to the sick and injured and helping deliver the babies who were born during the trip.

When the Smith party joined the wagon train led by John Brown, there were fifty-six white people and thirty-four slaves. "All things being ready," Brown wrote in his journal, "we started on the 10th of March in wet, muddy weather." The first day they went four miles, other days they covered as much as five times that distance. On March 21, Brown wrote, "Last night it rained and this morning is very rainy. . . . It was so wet and disagreeable. . . . Some three miles from our camp it assumed the character of a hurricane." In Paducah, Kentucky, they boarded a steamboat and traveled up the Mississippi River to St. Louis, Missouri. "We were . . . well prepared to appreciate it," Brown wrote, "having traveled in mud and rain, and camping in wagons and tents for one month." From St. Louis, they continued by land and encountered more difficult days, according to Brown's account:

June 1: "The wind blows so today that it is impossible to cross [the Missouri River]. Night before last, the wolves caught a sheep belonging to our camp and last night they killed a calf close by."

August 29: "We reached the Black Hills, where we found little or no feed, and our cattle began to die."

September 1: "We had a heavy storm of sleet. . . . At Bear River [near the border of Wyoming and Utah] we had quite a snowstorm, covering the ground several inches."

Finally, in mid-October, they reached their destination, after traveling almost seven months and well over a thousand miles.

Three years later, in 1851, Robert Smith, with his family and slaves, joined a wagon train of Mormons headed to San Bernardino, California, to start a new community. The journey of over nine hundred miles took them across the Mojave Desert and the San Bernardino Mountains. Biddy Mason, as before, walked and herded the livestock. This walk, however, took her to just the right place at just the right time because, the year before, California had become a state, a free state where slavery was no longer legal. Smith may not have known this when he decided to settle in California, or he may have heard that the new law was not always enforced. After a few years, however, as antislavery feelings grew stronger in California, Smith may have feared that he would be forced to free his slaves. So he decided to head for Texas, a state where slavery was legal and he could keep his slaves.

"I Always Feared This Trip to Texas"

This is when knowledge and love intervened to help Biddy Mason. The knowledge was the news that California was a free state. Mason undoubtedly heard that from free black people who lived in San Bernardino, in particular her friend Elizabeth Rowan. The love was between Biddy Mason's seventeen-year-old daughter Ellen and Charles Owens. Charles's father, Robert, a free black man who lived in Los Angeles, was a successful *vaquero*, or cowboy, and a businessman.

Mason told Elizabeth Rowan about Smith's plan that would end her chance to be free. She also told Charles who told his father. In the meantime, Smith's departure was delayed because Hannah was about to have her eighth child and could not travel. Suspecting that Mason might be seeking to free herself and her family, Smith took his family and slaves and camped out in a canyon in the Santa Monica Mountains to hide from the authorities. At that point, Elizabeth Rowan and Robert Owens sprang into action and got a writ of *habeas corpus*, a legal document used to protect a person from being held illegally.

Armed with this document and backed up by a group of vaqueros, Robert Owens and the sheriff rode into Smith's camp and told him that he could not leave until a judge heard the case. The sheriff took Mason and most of her family and put them in his jail to protect them from Smith until Judge Benjamin Hayes of the Los Angeles District Court issued his decision.

During the trial, Smith's lawyer told Judge Hayes that Biddy Mason and her family, including Hannah and her children, were members of Smith's family, not slaves. That they had left Mississippi of their own free will. That Smith "has supported them ever since, subjecting them to no greater control than his own children, and not holding them as slaves." That "It is understood, between said Smith and said persons that they will return to said State of Texas with him voluntarily, as a portion of his family."

Under California law, black people, mulattos, and Native Americans could not testify against white people, so Judge Hayes listened to Biddy Mason in his private chambers. "I always feared this trip to Texas, since I first heard of it," she told Hayes. "Mr. Smith told me I would be just as free in Texas as here." Thus, Mason bravely exposed Smith's lie. In addition to lying, Smith and his lawyer had bribed the lawyer for Mason and the others to drop the case, as well as apparently threatened Mason and Hannah. The judge discovered all this, including the fact that a member of Smith's party tried to kidnap two slave children while the trial was in progress.

After hearing the case for three days, Judge Hayes ruled that "all of the said persons of color are entitled to their freedom and are free forever." At last, Biddy Mason and thirteen members of her family were free, in the words of Judge Hayes, "to become settled and go to work for themselves—in peace and without fear." Mason won her case in 1856, just in time because in 1857 the U.S. Supreme Court's infamous ruling in the Dred Scott case invalidated any laws that allowed slaves to become free when they moved to free states or territories.

Biddy Mason started her life as a free woman at the age of thirty-seven. She and her family stayed with Robert Owens and his wife, Winnie, and their children, Charles, Sarah Jane, and Martha, in Los Angeles. Charles and Ellen got married and later had two sons, Robert and Henry.

Biddy Mason went to work as a midwife and nurse for Dr. John Strother Griffin, a friend of the Owens's. Los Angeles was growing fast; just as fast, Mason was gaining a reputation as a skilled healer and midwife. As always, she was brave. She went to prisons to care for sick inmates and tended to people during an epidemic of smallpox.

For thirty-five years, Biddy Mason carried her big black midwife's bag packed with supplies and delivered babies of all races and ethnicities, rich and poor. "She was always in demand as a midwife," wrote one observer, "and as such brought into the world many of the children of the early pioneer families." As was common, she was paid in cash by some people, with food or livestock such as a chicken by others. Like most midwives, Biddy Mason was called "Grandma" or "Aunt."

By 1866, Mason had saved enough money—$250—to buy property, although she continued to live in a rental house. At first, it appears that she built a house on her property and rented it to other people. Later she built a two-story building at 331 Spring Street and rented out the first floor to various businesses while living on the second floor. After her grandsons started a successful livery stable on part of the property, Mason deeded it to them for "the sum of love and affection and ten dollars." Her wealth grew as she continued to work and live frugally and buy and sell property.

"The Open Hand"

In 1872, Biddy Mason held a meeting in her home to organize the Los Angeles branch of the First African Methodist Episcopal Church, a large and thriving church to this day. In the 1880s, she responded to the needs of families who lost their homes in floods by paying for their groceries at a local grocery store. "Her home at No. 331 South Spring Street in later years," wrote one historian, "became a refuge for stranded and needy settlers. As she grew more feeble it became necessary for her grandson to stand at the gate each morning and turn away the line which had formed awaiting her assistance." Many years later, her great-granddaughter, Gladys Owens Smith, recalled Mason telling her, "If you hold your hand closed, Gladys, nothing good can come in. The open hand is blessed, for it gives in abundance, even as it receives."

Biddy Mason died in her home in 1891. Her funeral was held

at her church, and she was widely mourned. Then she was buried in a grave that remained unmarked until 1988, when the mayor of Los Angeles and three thousand members of the church that Mason founded surrounded her grave to dedicate a stone hailing her as a philanthropist and humanitarian. "She is an example of the courage of black women in the early days of this city," said Mayor Tom Bradley. "Our young people need to know about her."

Mason had admonished her children that the first piece of property she bought between Spring Street and Fort Street (later Broadway) and between Third and Fourth Street "was always to remain as their homestead, and it mattered not what their circumstances, they were always to retain this homestead." By the early 1980s, however, Mason's property had been turned into a parking lot, and her life story was for the most part forgotten. That all changed in the late 1980s. African American history and women's history were being celebrated, as were the stories of ordinary Americans—midwives, farmers, factory workers, teachers. Historians and architects and artists and urban planners and others were promoting public history through exhibits, documentaries, memorials, and events that brought history to places where people lived and worked. Foundations were offering funding to such organizations as The Power of Place in Los Angeles, which headed the effort to build the memorial to Biddy Mason on the site of her property.

Four of Biddy Mason's relatives attended the opening ceremony for the memorial: her ninety-five-year-old great-granddaughter Gladys Owens Smith and Robert Smith's great-granddaughter, Linda Cox. Cox's two daughters, Cheryl, age eleven, and Robynn, age nine, cut the ceremonial ribbon. "It took 100 years for Biddy Mason to be recognized," said Cox, "but we walk a lot taller knowing this history."

Biddy Mason's descendants at the dedication of the memorial.

CHAPTER EIGHT

"To Be Somebody"

PEGGY HULL: RESOLUTE REPORTER

1889–1967

PEGGY HULL'S parents did not name her Peggy Hull. They named her Henrietta Eleanor Goodnough. So how did she get to be Peggy Hull? She became Hull when she married George Hull and changed her name to Henrietta Goodnough Hull. This was the name she used when she started her career as a newspaper reporter. That lasted until a newspaper editor told her to come up with a new name because he "wouldn't be caught dead putting at the head of any column in his newspaper a name such as Henrietta Goodnough Hull."

From an early age, Henrietta was "determined to be somebody." She chose to try to make her mark in journalism because, as a child, she was inspired by reading about Nellie Bly and Richard Harding Davis. Both of them were pioneers: Bly as an investigative reporter and Davis as a war correspondent. Both were daring and skilled journalists, who excelled at descriptive writing. Both had a flare for flamboyance.

Henrietta dropped out of high school when she was sixteen years old, and, within a few years, she got her first newspaper job at the *Sentinel* in Bennington, Kansas. During the next seven years, she married George Hull, who was also a reporter, and, with her husband, moved to jobs at newspapers in Denver, Colorado; San Francisco, California; and Honolulu, Hawaii.

Peggy Hull, about 1910.

In Hawaii, Hull got fed up with George's heavy drinking (especially after he removed all his clothes and climbed a flagpole), and she left him. Moving to Minneapolis, Minnesota, she went to work for the *Daily News* and covered courtroom trials. Her articles had titles such as "Barred from Room of Dying Husband Mrs. Rogers Says" and "Auto Gives Clue to Murderer of Taxi-Cab Driver."

In 1916, she got a job at the *Cleveland Plain Dealer* and moved to Cleveland, Ohio. That was the year that the United States government sent troops, commanded by General John Pershing, into Mexico to capture Francisco "Pancho" Villa in retaliation for a raid Villa and his men had conducted on a town in New Mexico. In addition, National Guard troops were ordered to go and guard the long border between Mexico and the United States. The Fifth regiment of the Ohio National Guard was ordered to go to El Paso, Texas. When she heard that, Peggy Hull seized the opportunity to go to El Paso, too. She had always been fascinated by the military; she would have been a soldier, if she had been a man, she once said.

Peggy Hull was an energetic, athletic extrovert. A short, spunky woman, she had big, dark, highly expressive eyes and curly brown hair. She was as comfortable wearing a pink crepe de chine nightgown as she was wearing a "pearl gray woolen skirt and flannel shirt, a heavy pair of rubber soled shoes and a campaign hat." The tone of her writing was often as exuberant and engaging as she was. A photograph of her wearing a uniform she borrowed from the Ohio National Guard, her right hand raised in a salute, appeared beside her articles in the newspaper.

When a male reporter from the *Cleveland Plain Dealer* arrived and replaced her, Hull was undaunted. She got another job with a Texas paper, the *El Paso Herald*, then she moved on to the *El Paso Morning Times*.

"I Couldn't Quit"

Hull excelled at what is now called "networking." She developed contacts with other correspondents and military men, and not just by socializing, but by proving she could stand hardships. To that end, she convinced a general to let her go on a fifteen-day hike along with twenty thousand soldiers. "I had a terrible time convincing him I could stand the hardships," Hull wrote. "When I finally gained his consent, I knew my military career depended upon [that] hike." She "came through like [a] hardened veteran," she said, despite agonizing pain in her feet and her whole body at times, unbearable heat, and an intense sandstorm:

Water wagons were overturned in the desert or else lost their way and wandered from the main column. The wind raged and blinded us with fine white sand. We had no luncheon and no dinner. About one o'clock in the morning after the storm had spent itself, our weary field kitchen staggered into camp and . . . turned out food—and such food. Sanded bacon—sanded bread—sanded coffee sweetened with sanded sand.

I felt as though I had never had a bath. My hair was bristling and hard to sleep on. I didn't want a military career then, but I had convinced the general I did want one and I couldn't quit.

General John Pershing spent eleven months in Mexico chasing, but not capturing, Pancho Villa. Finally, Pershing led his army back across the border. Peggy Hull was there when they arrived, and her article, "Pershing's Ten Thousand Back from Mexico, Silent, Swarthy and Strong," was on the front page of the El Paso Morning Times. Her article continued on page four under a large photograph of Hull wearing a uniform and riding

Peggy Rides at Head of Cavalcade of Distinguished United States Army Officers

PERSHING'S TEN THOUSAND BACK FROM MEXICO, SILENT SWATHY AND STRONG

GONZALEZ SLAIN IN BATTLE IS REPORT

Former Juarez Commander Said to Have Died in Battle at La Cruz, Starting Sunday.

North Carolina Boys and Mexicans Across River Exchange Fire

BOY'S ATTEMPT TO CROSS STREET FATAL

Juan Padilla, 11 Years Old, Dies as Result of Being Hurled to Pavement by Truck.

Republican Praises Work of Aldermen O'Connor and Stevens

ONLY 2 AMERICAN STEAMERS AT SEA

Philadelphia and Finland Arrive at Liverpool and St. Paul Anchors Off Sandy Hook.

Labor Congress Names Committee to Draw Up Necessary Constitution

The newspaper article that appeared in the El Paso Morning Times.

a horse in front of General Pershing and his troops! A headline above the picture reads, "Peggy Rides at Head of Cavalcade of Distinguished United States Army Officers." One of Hull's close friends, Irene Corbally Kuhn, later explained that it was a stunt set up by a movie cameraman:

> When word came that the General was riding out at the head of the troops, . . . the newsreel men were tipped off that the best pix were to be had at a certain spot. Peggy was spirited to the rendezvous on her horse, and kept out of sight. At precisely the right moment, as . . . General Pershing appeared on his charger, and just a moment before the newsreel camera started to grind, the signal was given. Peggy trotted her horse into position, alongside the General, the newsreel camera started whirring, the troops cheered, and the pictures appeared all over the U.S. and the world: "American girl correspondent leads troops out of Mexico with General Pershing."

In April 1917, two months after Pershing and his troops left Mexico, the United States entered World War I, which had been raging in Europe for several years. General Pershing was named the commander of the American Expeditionary Forces in France. Determined to be a war correspondent, Peggy Hull asked the managing editor of the *Morning News* to send her to France.

"How perfectly ridiculous! . . . It would cost too much money, even if you could get a passport, which I am sure you couldn't," he said with "scorn in his voice."

She kept talking, until, finally, he agreed. Now, she needed to convince American officials to issue her a passport and British and French officials to issue her visas.

The American and French officials were accommodating. However, she later wrote that the British official was a "thick set, square-faced, heavily spectacled man" who looked at her "with open disapproval."

"What do you know about military affairs—what can you write about modern warfare—what has been your experience as a war correspondent?" he asked her.

"I've been on the Mexican border for the past eight months. I've made hikes with Major General Morton and his command, and I wrote a story about Major General Pershing's return from Mexico," she replied.

"Before I visa this passport, I will have to know what type of newspaper you are writing for and the kind of stories you write. You are entering a military area and I must be satisfied as to your real qualifications to be there. . . . Have you ever been abroad?"

"No."

"You've never been abroad before and now your paper is sending you over there as a correspondent?"

"Yes," Hull replied.

Finally, Peggy Hull supplied the man with copies of the newspapers with her articles. After scrutinizing them, he "fumbled around for stamps and pen and ink," and issued her the visa.

She arrived in England on June 25, after a twelve-day voyage through submarine-infested waters. She was lacking an official U.S. war correspondent's pass because the United States government refused to accredit women. Nevertheless, she set off to cover the American troops in France.

She scored a coup when General Pershing agreed to an interview. "He appeared glad to see me," she reported. "And I remembered the day . . . when he rode out of Mexico not so crisp, not so well groomed as now. . . . At first I was a bit afraid

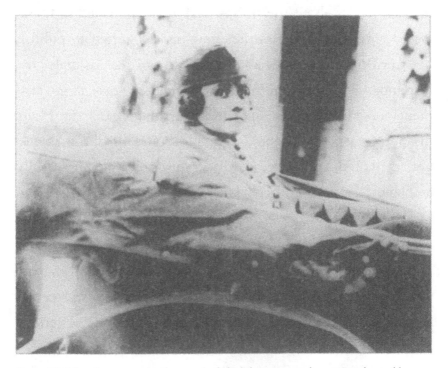

Peggy Hull loved wearing a uniform and relished the attention she got. People would crowd around her to get a closer look at her boots and hat, and even to count the number of buttons on her jacket. This picture was taken in Paris, France, in 1917.

that the great general might say this was no place for a girl correspondent and that I'd have to go home."

"Why, Peggy! How in the world did you get over here—you
don't mean to say you came all alone?" he asked.

"Yes—all alone—all the way from El Paso just so the people
on the border could have news of you from one of their home
folks," she explained.

"I'm glad you are here," he said. . . . "I'm sure all the men will
appreciate it. . . . You are a long ways from home—but you
mustn't be scared—we'll see that you get along all right."

She got along fine, for a while. She wrote lively human-
interest stories about the troops that were published in the *El
Paso Morning Times*. Then other newspapers started to publish
her stories, too. Her success prompted some jealous male correspondents to complain that she did not have official government accreditation like they did. Pershing, much to Hull's
disappointment, did nothing to help her, and, finally, unable to
get accredited, Hull was forced to return to Texas. "It is really
a shame I have to go back now," she wrote, but added, "no
one can ever take this—the greatest adventure of my life—
from me."

In the summer of 1918, Peggy Hull went to Washington,
D.C., and doggedly set out to get accredited as a war correspondent. While she was there, she heard about an American
military expedition that was going to Siberia to protect Czech-
oslovakian troops that were stuck there in the aftermath of
the Russian Revolution. She went to see General Peyton

March, an old contact and friend, who was now stationed in Washington.

According to Hull, March said, "Your stories are the sort that give the people at home a real idea of what the American soldier is like and what he likes and dislikes. I'd like to see you go with the Siberian expedition. . . . If you can get an editor to send you, I'll accredit you!"

Although it took her several weeks, Hull finally found an editor who would send her. But Captain Ruth, who was in charge of issuing the war correspondent's pass, refused her. "No woman shall be accredited," he said. With that, Hull went back to see General March and returned with an order signed by him: "If your only reason for refusing Miss Peggy Hull credentials is because she is a woman, issue them at once and facilitate her procedure to Vladivostok."

Peggy Hull's pass, the first one ever given to a woman by the War Department, was an eight-by-eleven-inch piece of heavy vellum paper with her signature and photograph. It read:

The Bearer, Miss Peggy (Henrietta G.) Hull, whose photograph and signature are hereto attached, is hereby accredited to the Commanding General, American Expeditionary Forces, Siberia, United States Army, as news correspondent of the Newspaper Enterprise Association with permission to accompany said troops, subject to the Regulations governing Correspondents with Troops in the Field and the orders of the commander of said troops.

This pass entitles the correspondent to passage on military railways and, when accommodations are available, on Army transports, with the privileges of a commissioned officer, including purchase of subsistence, forage and indispensable supplies when they can be spared.

"Sex Counts for Nothing"

Peggy Hull spent seven very cold and frustrating months in Siberia, most of them in Vladivostok. The political turmoil inside Russia was exacerbated by interference from foreign soldiers—Japanese, Canadian, Polish, Serbian, Italian, Czech, British, and American. "I was in command of the . . . troops," wrote Major General William Graves, leader of the American Expeditionary Forces, "and, I must admit, I do not know what the United States was trying to accomplish."

Under difficult circumstances, Peggy Hull reported as best she could. All in all, however, her experience as the first woman accredited war correspondent was disheartening. For one thing, Graves restricted her movements until she contacted General March. He wrote to Graves, "Of course you understand that sex counts for nothing in this modern game and Miss Hull is like any other newspaper correspondent in regard to being permitted to see whatever you let any one else see. No favors to be shown her, but on the other hand, no repression either." In addition, she witnessed unbecoming behavior on the part of soldiers that unsettled her idealized view of the military.

Hull left Siberia for the United States in June 1919. In the following years, she got divorced from George Hull and married an English ship captain, John Kinley, which meant she was no longer a U.S. citizen because of the United States law at that time, which stipulated that a woman lost her American citizenship when she married an alien man. Hull eventually helped change that law. (She also eventually got divorced from John Kinley.) She wrote magazine articles and traveled and worked for newspapers in Shanghai, China. She was there when the Japanese attacked in 1932.

When word of the attack reached New York City, an editor at the *New York Daily News* who knew Hull was in Shanghai sent her a cable with these instructions: "Go to work; you're our correspondent."

She went without sleep for three days. For the next thirty days, she slept sitting in a chair. At one point, she climbed to the roof of the tallest building in the International Settlement, the area of Shanghai where foreigners lived, and stood "for three hours watching the planes drop their bombs. . . . I saw the resultant flames destroy hundreds of tenement homes in Chapei, where dwell close to 1,000,000 Chinese laborers. The tenements crumbled like pie crusts and the ruins burst into flames as the terrified Chinese fled into the narrow streets. . . . Thousands huddled in the debris. It was a frightful scene of human misery."

Because the United States was a neutral nation, both sides

Admiral Kichisaburo Nomura gave Peggy Hull a copy of this photograph that was taken during her visit to his flagship Idzumo *during the Shanghai war in 1932.*

were eager to present their cases to American correspondents. Admiral Kichisaburo Nomura invited Peggy Hull to have dinner aboard the *Idzumo*, the flagship of the Japanese fleet. She reported that he "pretended to admire the vitality of American women, but . . . he felt that the Japanese women were superior to American women because psychologically they gave their vitality to men."

Hull left the ship with a picture of Nomura, which he inscribed to her, and a safe-conduct pass. Hull described the pass as "a piece of unbleached muslin, a square not much larger than [her] hand. In one corner . . . was a red symbol. It was . . . an Oriental design stamped on the cloth. Running down the right side were big black characters." As Nomura had handed the pass to her, he had said, "If you are ever in danger with Japanese troops, show this. You are the only foreigner to whom we are giving this type of identification."

"Sasha Fell Dead"

Hull had to go through a war zone to interview the commander of the Chinese Nineteenth Route Army, General Tsai

Ting-kai. She hired a car with a Russian driver, Sasha, who was also considered a neutral. Heavy cross fire broke out, and Hull and Sasha abandoned their car, taking cover in an above-ground, mound-shaped Chinese tomb. Around them, they saw Chinese soldiers in retreat. Sasha panicked and bolted from the tomb toward the oncoming Japanese soldiers, whose rifles were "smoking at exact intervals." Sasha fell dead.

As the soldiers advanced, Hull suddenly remembered her safe-conduct pass. She searched her purse. She dumped everything out and pawed through the contents—no pass. Finally she found it folded neatly in her passport. Figuring that the soldiers would aim for her heart, she pinned the pass with hairpins over her left breast. Hoping the soldiers would notice that her coat and beret were tan, not gray like the Chinese uniforms, Hull crawled out of the tomb and stood up with her arms raised above her head. Facing the soldiers, she later wrote, she "felt a curious, quieting comradeship with them. They, too, might be about to die; they, too, might be walking in the last moments of their lives."

The soldiers stopped. According to Hull:

Not more than twenty paces separated us. As the lieutenant moved toward me, his revolver in his hand, I walked out to meet him. I made no effort to speak but with my right hand, I pointed to the muslin identification tag on my coat. . . .

His eyes rested on it. . . . Slowly . . . he bowed toward me, respectfully and obediently. . . .

"You are lost?" he asked. . . .

I replied slowly, trying to control my voice, "I did not mean to come here. I did not know there was fighting."

He spoke kindly, "You are safe. Three of my men will take you to headquarters. General Shirakawa will send you to your hotel." . . .

This was more than I had hoped for or expected. . . . [To] be taken to headquarters and provided with a motor car and escort only equaled my astonishment at the thought of meeting General Shirakawa again. We had last met in Siberia.

When I entered his office two hours later, shaken and unable to conceal the ragged edges of my fright, he thoughtfully recalled our last meeting at an Allied tea party in Vladivostok in 1919. He smiled at me, his brown eyes twinkling in friendliness and relief.

"You know," he said softly, "if you do not give up your war corresponding, you are surely going to end your life on a battlefield."

Day after day, Peggy Hull filed dispatches. Here are excerpts of her descriptive writing:

February 1—Thousands of refugees crowded the streets. A cold rain fell upon them as they huddled, like stray animals, in doorways, alleyways, the lee of buildings.

February 2—I visited the Buddhist temple on Bubbling Well Road today, which has been converted into a receiving station for the wounded in last Friday's aerial attack. . . .

It was mercifully dusk under the venerable roof—raised a thousand years ago by a wandering band of Buddha's disciples, who had found the waters of the Bubbling Well sweet.

In the air heavy with smoldering joss and before altars hung with paper streamers in red and gold, descendants of those priests continued the gentle service. . . .

But the floors were covered with ragged refugees, wounded, dying. . . . They lay, some of them, in pools of blood. . . .

It is impossible to use the side-walks because of the masses of gray-robed, black-trousered women who move aimlessly about, with their children whimpering at their heels.

February 3—But tragic as is the plight of the wounded, still more tragic are the orphaned and homeless children who wander like lost dogs just outside the fighting zone. Pitiful scenes are enacted as they plead for someone to find their parents.

A small blind boy had clung to an iron grating since Sunday. He was crying with hunger and terror when his small hands were loosened, and he was borne to safety. None can guess his mother's fate.

February 21—Unburied dead littered the shell-pitted streets of the No Man's Land. . . .

Three Japanese planes loitered in the sky. Like careful seamstresses, sewing to a line, they dropped their bombs on the rabbit warrens where the Chinese troops huddled. . . .

The fighting stopped on March 3. Under pressure from other countries, Japan withdrew from some of the areas it had captured. This experience, Peggy Hull later said, "made a veteran out of me." She later wrote that, like many veterans, "I still suffer from the noise and terror. . . . A door slamming violently makes me tremble before I have a chance to remember that it isn't a shell or a bomb. I dread the sound of airplanes overhead and do not believe I will ever get over that feeling."

A year later, in 1933, she married a wealthy, influential newspaper editor, Harvey Deuell. He died in 1939, the same year World War II started in Europe. When the United States entered the war in 1941, Peggy Hull was determined to cover it, and she did, despite being more than fifty years old. She was stationed in the Pacific and reported from Hawaii, Guam, Tarawa, and Saipan. As always, she wrote human-interest pieces about ordinary soldiers. The soldiers showed their appreciation by giving her badges and patches that represented their particular outfit. Private Frederick White of Wellington, Ohio, who was later killed in the war, gave her the first one.

Hull proudly sewed the badge on the beret she always wore. By the time the war was over, she had eight berets covered with fifty badges. The U.S. Navy awarded her a commendation for her service during the war.

World War II was Peggy Hull's last war. After that she lived a quiet life and died in 1967. Although she is not well-known now, Peggy Hull did become somebody, at least in the hearts of the soldiers she wrote about. In the words of one soldier, "You made them know they weren't forgotten."

VERY BRIEF CHRONOLOGIES

Louise Boyd

1887 Born in San Francisco, California, on September 16.

1931 Leads the first of what will be seven expeditions into the Arctic.

1935 Publishes the first of several books about her expeditions, including a photographic trip she took to Poland in 1934.

1938 Becomes the second woman to receive the Cullum Medal of the American Geographical Society.

1972 Cremated remains dropped from a plane over the ice of the Arctic Ocean.

Mary Gibson Henry

1884 Born in Jenkintown, Pennsylvania, on August 15.

1928 Begins plant hunting.

1930 Leads the first of what will be four plant-hunting expeditions to northern British Columbia.

1948 Gives a series of lectures in Great Britain and is awarded the Mungo Park Medal from the Royal Scottish Geographical Society.

1967 Dies in Wilmington, North Carolina, while hunting plants on April 16.

Juana Briones

1802 Born in Branciforte (now Santa Cruz), California.

1820 Marries Apolinario Miranda.

1830s Acquires property in Yerba Buena, now San Francisco.

1844 Purchases Rancho la Purisima Concepción.

1889 Dies in San Francisco on December 3.

Alice Hamilton

1869   Born in New York City on February 27.

1908   Begins investigating industrial poisons.

1919   Becomes the first woman professor at Harvard University.

1943   Publishes her autobiography, *Exploring the Dangerous Trades*.

1970   Dies in Hadlyme, Connecticut, on September 22.

Mary McLeod Bethune

1875   Born near Mayesville, South Carolina, on July 10.

1904   Founds her school, known today as Bethune-Cookman College.

1935   Founds the National Council of Negro Women and is awarded the Spingarn Medal by the National Association for the Advancement of Colored People.

1936   Appointed director of the National Youth Administration's Division of Negro Affairs by President Franklin Roosevelt.

1955   Dies in Daytona Beach, Florida, on May 18.

Katharine Wormeley

1830   Born in Ipswich, Suffolk, England, on January 14.

1848   Immigrates with family to the United States.

1861   Civil War begins. Wormeley helps form local Women's Union Aid Society.

1862   Serves on the hospital transport ships from May through July.

1908   Dies in Jackson, New Hampshire, on August 4.

Biddy Mason

1818   Born a slave, possibly in Georgia, on August 15.

1848 & 1851   Walks to Utah, then to California, behind a wagon train.

1856   Wins her freedom in court and begins working as a midwife.

1866   Buys land and builds a homestead for herself and her family.

1891   Dies in Los Angeles, California, on January 15.

Peggy Hull

1889   Born Henrietta Eleanor Goodnough on a farm near Bennington, Kansas.

1905   Leaves school at the age of sixteen and gets her first newspaper job.

1918   Becomes the first woman to be accredited as a war correspondent by the U.S. government.

1932   Covers the Japanese attack on Shanghai for the *New York Daily News*.

1967   Dies in Carmel, California, on June 19.

PLACES TO VISIT

Louise Boyd

- Maple Lawn, former Boyd estate (now Elks Club Lodge #1108), 1312 Mission Avenue, San Rafael, California
- Miss Boyd Land, also called Louise Boyd Land, Northeast Greenland, latitude 73° 30' N, 27° 30' W (pictures and journal entries of the Cambridge Greenland Glaciology Expedition 2002 to Louise Boyd Land are on the Internet at http://www.greenland 2002.org.uk/loc.html)
- Louise Boyd Exhibit, a virtual tour, Marin History Museum, San Rafael, California, http://www.marinhistory.org/tour.html
- Burial site, one hundred miles north of Point Barrow, Alaska

Mary Gibson Henry

- Mount Mary Henry, British Columbia, Canada
- Henry Foundation for Botanical Research, 801 Stony Lane, Gladwyne, Pennsylvania
- Burial site, Gladwyne, Pennsylvania

Juana Briones

- Plaque, northeast corner of Washington Square Park, San Francisco, California
- Archaeological excavation, El Polin Spring, Presidio, San Francisco, California
- Adobe Ranch House, Rancho la Purisima Concepción, 4155 Adobe Road, Palo Alto, California
- Burial site, Holy Cross Cemetery, Menlo Park, California

Alice Hamilton

- The National Women's Hall of Fame, 76 Fall Street, Seneca Falls, New York

- Edith and Alice Hamilton Dormitory, Connecticut College, New London, Connecticut
- Burial site, Hadlyme, Connecticut

Mary McLeod Bethune

- Marker near site of birthplace, Mayesville, South Carolina
- Mary McLeod Bethune Park, Mayesville, South Carolina
- Mary McLeod Bethune Council House, 1318 Vermont Avenue, N.W., Washington, D.C.
- Statue, Lincoln Park, East Capitol Street at 12th Street, S.E., Washington, D.C.
- Bethune Hall, Howard University, 4th and College Streets, N.W., Washington, D.C.
- Bethune-Cookman College (and Bethune's on-campus home), Second Avenue between McLeod and Lincoln Street, Daytona Beach, Florida
- South Carolina Hall of Fame, Myrtle Beach Convention Center, 21st Avenue North and Oak Street, Myrtle Beach, South Carolina
- The National Women's Hall of Fame, 76 Fall Street, Seneca Falls, New York
- Burial site, campus of Bethune-Cookman College, Daytona Beach, Florida

Katharine Wormeley

- Burial site, Island Cemetery, Newport, Rhode Island

Biddy Mason

- Biddy Mason's Place: A Passage of Time, a memorial in Biddy Mason Park, between Broadway and Spring Street at 3rd Street, Los Angeles, California
- Burial site, Evergreen Cemetery, Boyle Heights area of Los Angeles, California

Peggy Hull

- Peggy Hull Deuell Collection, Kenneth Spencer Research Library, 1450 Poplar Lane, University of Kansas, Lawrence, Kansas
- Burial site, Woodlawn Cemetery, New Windsor, New York

NAMESAKES

The names of some of the adventurous women can be found today attached to all sorts of things, including mountains, ice-covered land, plants and flowers, postage stamps, schools, and scholarships. Here is a partial list:

Louise Boyd

- Miss Boyd Land, also called Louise Boyd Land, Northeast Greenland
- Louise A. Bank, the ocean bottom between Bear Island and Jan Mayen Island, center latitude: 72.6833333; longitude: 2.9166667 (you can search for this location on a map at www.earthsearch.net)
- Louise Glacier, Northeast Greenland

Mary Gibson Henry

- Mount Mary Henry, British Columbia, Canada
- Numerous plants, including "Henry's Garnet" (*Itea virginia*) and *Phlox henryae*
- Henry Foundation for Botanical Research, Gladwyne, Pennsylvania

Juana Briones

- Juana Briones Elementary School, Palo Alto, California
- Juana Briones Heritage Foundation, Palo Alto, California

Alice Hamilton

- Alice Hamilton Fund for Occupational Health at the School of Public Health, Harvard University, Cambridge, Massachusetts
- Alice Hamilton Science Award for Occupational Safety and Health, National Institute for Occupational Safety and Health (NIOSH), Washington, D. C.
- Alice Hamilton Laboratory, NIOSH, Cincinnati, Ohio

- Her likeness was featured on a United States postage stamp in the "Great American" series

Mary McLeod Bethune

- Dr. Mary McLeod Bethune Elementary School, Riviera Beach, Florida
- Her likeness was featured on a United States postage stamp in the "Great American" series
- Mary McLeod Bethune Park, Mayesville, South Carolina
- Mary McLeod Bethune Middle School, Los Angeles, California
- Bethune-Cookman College, Daytona Beach, Florida
- Bethune Hall (dormitory), Howard University, Washington, D.C.

ACKNOWLEDGMENTS

As always, my family was a source of indispensable love and support. My love and thanks forever. I also thank Christy Ottaviano, the perfect editor, and everyone at Henry Holt who worked on this book. Numerous people provided information and photographs, and I thank them, too, including Jeanne Farr McDonnell, founder of the Women's Heritage Museum, now the International Museum of Women, San Francisco, California; Bob Knapp, Palo Alto, California; Steve Staiger, Palo Alto Historical Association, Palo Alto, California; Melanie Cross, Juana Briones Heritage Foundation, Palo Alto, California; Madelyn Crawford, Los Altos History Museum, Los Altos, California; Jacalyn Blume, Schlesinger Library, Radcliffe Institute for Advanced Study, Cambridge, Massachusetts; Susan Pepper Treadway and Betsey Warren Davis, Henry Foundation for Botanical Research, Gladwyne, Pennsylvania; and Kathy Lafferty, Kenneth Spencer, Research Library, University of Kansas Libraries, Lawrence, Kansas.

Permission to quote from the following is gratefully acknowledged:

Exploring the Dangerous Trades by Alice Hamilton, © 1985 by Northeastern University Press.

Fiord Region of East Greenland, © 1935, and *The Coast of Northeast Greenland,* © 1948, by Louise Boyd, American Geographical Society.

"Mary Gibson Henry: An Autobiography" by Mary Gibson Henry, © 1950, *Plant Life,* American Horticultural Society.

The Power of Place by Dolores Hayden, © 1997, MIT Press.

SOURCE NOTES

Complete information about the sources is given in the bibliography, page 175.

Louise Boyd

Abbreviations used are: Boyd Fiord—*The Fiord Region of East Greenland,* Boyd Coast—*The Coast of Northeast Greenland*

Page
9   "Cold? Yes . . . it": Sherr and Kazickas, p. 52.

            "first . . . north": Boyd Coast, p. 1.

10   "see . . . ice": Boyd Fiord, p. 2.

            "begged . . . cajoled": Owen, p. 6.

10–11 "could smell . . . Nothing": ibid.

11   "I had . . . back": ibid.

            "tall . . . elegant": Olds, p. 235.

11–12 "I had . . . cool": "American Girl Shot 11 Bears in Arctic," *New York Times,* p. E1.

12   "jagged peaks . . . lands": Boyd Fiord, p. 1.

            "I revel . . . again": "American Girl Shot 11 Bears in Arctic," *New York Times,*
               p. E1.

13   "We felt . . . Amundsen": Boyd Coast, p. 1.

            "Four of . . . more": Stefoff, p. 116.

14   "some 10,000 . . . Sea": Boyd Coast, p 1.

            "Folks . . . good-bye": "Arctic Search Fun for Marin 'Tomboy,' " *San Rafael
               Independent,* p. 31.

14–15 "every fiord . . . valley walls": Boyd Fiord, p. 2.

15   "needed . . . water": Boyd Coast, p. 88.

16   "The reward . . . beauty": Boyd Fiord, p. 2.

            "knowledge of . . . ice": ibid., p. 1.

            "suited . . . along fine": Owen, p. 6.

17   "I like . . . sea is": quoted in Curtis, "Louise Arner Boyd Dies at 84," p. 66.

18   "railed under . . . feat": Boyd Fiord, p. 6.

            "You hear . . . fiords": ibid., p. 54.

19   "Inanimate nature . . . rocks": ibid., p. 34.

            "Nature was . . . condition": ibid., pp. 40–41.

20   "loomed up . . . sunlight": Boyd Coast, p. 9.

            "all-important . . . ice": ibid., p. 11.

20   "a tantalizing . . . coast": ibid.

22   "I have . . . it": Boyd Coast, p. 74.

23–24   "prospective photographers . . . got me": ibid., p. 88.

24–25   "North, north . . . ice": Olds, p. 291.

25   "I don't . . . dentist": Curtis, "Society Glitters," p. 41.

Mary Gibson Henry

Abbreviations used are: MGH—"Mary Gibson Henry: An Autobiography"; Henry—"Collecting Plants Beyond the Frontier," January 1934

Page

26   "gem . . . treasures": MGH, p. 11.

27   "As a . . . ooze": ibid.

          "His influence . . . me": MGH, p. 11.

27–28   "The magnificence . . . experience": ibid.

28   "some Lilacs . . . greenhouse": ibid., p. 12.

28–29   "Great grief . . . to do": ibid.

30   "These intrepid . . . nation": "The Impact of the Plant-hunters," Royal Botanic
          Garden Edinburgh [http://www.rbge.org.uk/rbge/web/news/
          planthunt.jsp].

          "It was . . . earned it all": MGH, p. 23.

          "insulated . . . comfortably": ibid.

31   "My first . . . successful": ibid., p. 12.

31–32   "I soon learned . . . high": ibid., pp. 12–13.

32   "The eastern . . . bad at all": ibid., p. 13.

33   "wanted to . . . plants": Henry, unpaged.

          "We were advised . . . to go": ibid.

          "There was . . . for me": ibid.

34   "A Victrola . . . mountainside": ibid.

35   "thrown wide . . . not at all": ibid.

          "For the first . . . beautiful": ibid.

          "Whenever I . . . me": ibid.

36   "aired . . . chop them loose": ibid.

          "The grandeur . . . fragance": ibid.

36–37   "We preferred . . . good progress": ibid.

37   "We really . . . mires": ibid.

37–38   "pure, pale . . . pass": ibid.

38   "the most . . . snow": ibid.

          "a beautiful . . . transparent": ibid.

38–39   "tossed like . . . I fell": ibid.

39   "My heart . . . worthwhile": ibid.

          "To be honest . . . friends": ibid.

40	"We went . . . to fall": ibid.
	"really hurt . . . good-bye": ibid.
	"a great longing": MGH, p. 17.
40–42	"could hardly . . . behind it": ibid., p. 18.
42	"that magnificent country . . . time": ibid.
	"I watched . . . return": ibid., p. 20.
	"old longings . . . hundredfold": ibid.
43	"calling Mrs. Henry . . . core": ibid.
	"rode along . . . sounds": ibid.
	"September 13th I . . . bears": ibid., p. 22.
43–44	"fell over . . . various times": ibid.
44	"We had . . . time": ibid., p. 23.
	"The happy . . . us": ibid., p. 24.
44–45	"Georgia . . . snakes there": "Lady Botanist," *New Yorker*, July 27, 1963.
45	"race . . . August": MGH, p. 26.
	"As for the flowers . . . them": ibid.

Juana Briones

Abbreviations used are: Bowman—"Juana Briones de Miranda"; Fava—*Los Altos Hills*; Voss—"The Briones Sisters"

Page

48–49	"An old . . . him": Bowman, p. 230.
49–50	"The pioneers . . . satisfied": ibid., p. 227.
50	"this consisted . . . manner": Fava, p. 40.
51–54	"In the . . . anxious to taste": Bowman, pp. 233–35.
54	"I fear . . . example": Voss, p. 3.
55	"Being burdened . . . sell it": "Who's Juana?": [http://www.brioneshouse.org/juana.html].
56	"quite comfortable . . . dogs": Bowman, p. 237.
57	"She liked . . . ranching": ibid., p. 238.
58	"very tall . . . doña": ibid., p. 239.

Alice Hamilton

Abbreviations used are: AH—*Exploring the Dangerous Trades*, Hamilton's autobiography; Sicherman—*Alice Hamilton: A Life in Letters*

Page

61	"disgusting . . . butcher": Sicherman, p. 34.
	"As a . . . anywhere": AH, p. 38.
62	"endless hiding . . . everything": ibid., p. 26.

62–63   "Yet, in . . . defend it": ibid., pp. 29–30.

63   "The teaching . . . worst": ibid., p. 36.

"She gave . . . nonsense": ibid., p. 37.

"personal liberty . . . us": ibid., p. 32.

"hope of . . . world": ibid., p. 38.

"incomplete and scrappy": ibid., p. 35.

64   "Those were . . . eye": ibid., p. 40.

64–65   "Each new . . . and it worked": ibid., p. 43.

65   "She seemed . . . contemptible": ibid.

65–66   "I accepted . . . House": ibid., p. 53.

66   "The rule . . . immigrants": ibid., p. 45.

67   "In settlement . . . orphanage": ibid., p. 74.

"divide . . . them": Sicherman, p. 152.

"never . . . scientist": AH, p. 128.

"a fiery pen": ibid., p. 115.

68   "tales . . . stockyard": ibid.

68–69   "to the Crerar . . . American": ibid.

69   "That sort . . . workers": ibid.

70   "We were staggered . . . unknown": ibid., p. 119.

"wrist-drop . . . helplessly": Alice Hamilton, *Women in the Lead Industries* (Washington, D.C.: Government Printing Office, 1919), 7.

71   "unearth . . . poisoning": AH, p. 120.

"Thus I . . . tinfoil": ibid.

"A skeleton . . . expressionless": ibid., pp. 123–24.

"is brought . . . lead": ibid., p. 122.

"It was a . . . problem": ibid., p. 124.

73   "Interesting as . . . in it": ibid., p. 128.

"I never . . . measure": ibid., p. 129.

"The time . . . on": ibid., p. 128.

"almost fragile": Sicherman, p. 52.

"the tiresome . . . differently": ibid., p. 181.

74   "Negroes . . . a week": AH, p. 131.

"bleak day . . . you're there": ibid., pp. 145–46.

75   "who waited . . . men": ibid., pp. 146–47.

"the same . . . lead colic": ibid., p. 147.

"seamy side . . . progress": ibid.

76   "a member . . . speed": ibid., p. 158.

"damnable . . . dying": Bill Kovarik, "The Radium Girls": 7 [http://www.runet.edu/~wkovarik/hist1/radium.html].

77   "If there . . . canaries": AH, p. 184.

"with wide . . . out again": ibid., p. 185–86.

77–78   "It was . . . men": ibid., p. 186.

78   "It was not . . . abuse": ibid., p. 193.
        "great glass . . of it": ibid., p. 195.
        "industrial medicine . . . respectable": ibid., p. 198.

79   "climbing down . . . slipped": ibid., p. 217.
        "There was . . . acid": ibid., p. 213.
        "We think it . . . fair": ibid., pp. 220–21.
        "the stronghold . . . women": ibid., p. 252.

80   "It seemed . . . available": ibid., p. 252.
        "each year . . . platform": ibid., p. 253.
        "There are few . . . me": ibid., p. 389.

81   "The story . . . complete": ibid., p. 393.
        "half the . . . to the public": Sicherman, p. 372.

81–82   "My God . . . write": ibid.

82   "a little . . . she disapproves": ibid., p. 383.
        "We Hamiltons . . . watch": ibid., pp. 387–98.

82–84   "Perhaps . . . surface": Alice Hamilton, "A Woman of Ninety Looks at Her World," *Atlantic Monthly*, September 1961: 51.

84   "You see . . . life": Sicherman, p. 9.
        "Edith's name . . . place": ibid.
        "For me . . . of it": Edward T. James et al., eds., *Notable American Women: A Biographical Dictionary* (Cambridge, MA: The Belknap Press, 1971): 306.

Mary McLeod Bethune

Abbreviations used are: Bethune Faith—"Faith That Moved a Dump Heap"; Bethune Will—"My Last Will and Testament"; Peare—*Mary McLeod Bethune*

Page
85   "full . . . Negro": Bethune Will, p. 105.
87   "I . . . picker": Bethune Faith, p. 32.
        "The drums . . . heart": ibid.
88   "Put down . . . read": Peare, p. 28.
        "Please . . . read": ibid., p. 31.
        "changed my . . . me": Bethune Faith, p. 32.
        "Every . . . home": ibid.
        "I used . . . more": ibid., p. 33.
89   "taught that . . . thing": Peare, p. 57.
89–90   "I have . . . do": Bethune Will, p. 108.
90   "The greatest . . . days": Peare, p. 73.
        "From her . . . country": Bethune Faith, p. 33.
91   "got restless . . . people": ibid., p. 34.
        "Whenever . . . number": ibid.
        "a beautiful . . . pines": ibid.
92   "I found . . . discouraged": ibid.

93 "We burned . . . lumber": ibid.

  "As parents . . . hair": ibid.

94 "Strongly interracial": ibid., p. 35.

  "prayed . . . talked up": ibid.

  "I took . . . handerchief": ibid., p. 34.

  "Even my . . . beds" ibid., p. 35.

95 "no race . . . rise": Audrey Thomas McCluskey and Elaine M. Smith, eds.,

  Mary McLeod Bethune: Building a Better World (Bloomington: Indiana

  University Press, 2002): 49.

96 "If you . . . us": Peare, p. 137.

  "Oh, how . . . life": ibid., p. 77.

97 "The NYA . . . opportunity": ibid., p. 164.

  "Prejudice of . . . religion": Bethune Faith, p. 35.

99 "Sometimes as . . . realized": Bethune Will, p. 105.

99–100 "I leave . . . young people": ibid., pp. 105–10.

Katharine Wormeley

Abbreviations used are: KW—*The Other Side of War,* Wormeley's letters; GB—*Letters of a Family,* Georgeanna Bacon's letters

Page

101 "a whirlwind . . . work": KW, p. 97.

101–2 "Men in . . . wounded": ibid., pp. 103, 105.

102 "passionate . . . oppression": Wormeley et al., unpaged.

104 "If I . . . tonight": KW, p. 16.

105–6 "He is . . . occasionally)": ibid., pp. 62–63.

106 "efficient . . . light-hearted": ibid., p. 44.

106–7 "I have . . . minute": ibid., pp. 159–60.

107 "My dresses . . . supplies": ibid., pp. 164–65.

107–8 "We are . . . ten minutes": ibid., pp. 75–76.

108 "Of course . . . ladders": ibid., p. 92.

  "Such letters . . . home": ibid., p. 121.

  "great skedaddle": Jane Turner Censer, ed., *The Papers of Frederick Law Olmsted,*

  Vol. 4 of *Defending the Union: The Civil War and U.S. Sanitary Commission,*

  1861–1863 (Baltimore: The Johns Hopkins University Press): 316.

109 "Georgy . . . civilized": ibid., p. 205.

110 "Miss Wormeley . . . her": GB, vol. 2, p. 501.

111 "Remember . . . in life": Olmsted, p. 114.

  "a period . . . another": KW, p. 205.

112 "I write . . . else": ibid., pp. 16–17.

113 "Transferred . . . tea": ibid., pp. 20–21.

113–14 "Yours . . . funny": ibid., pp. 25–26.

115   "We all . . . so": ibid., pp. 33–35.

115–16   "After dinner . . . wounded": ibid., pp. 46–47.

116   "The weather . . . week": ibid., pp. 58–59.

116–17   "We go . . . gold": ibid., pp. 69–70.

117   "It is . . . feeling it": ibid., pp. 77–78.

117–18   "The long . . . letter": ibid., pp. 92–93.

118–19   "I write . . . pouring in": ibid., pp. 95–96.

119   "What a . . . cost": , pp. 97–98, 101.

120   "We went . . . passed": ibid., pp. 103–4, 108, 111.

          "This is . . . somewhere": ibid., pp. 111, 114, 115.

121   "I can't . . . soul": ibid., pp. 121–22.

121–22   "I hope . . . Tuesday": ibid., pp. 137–38.

122   "Yesterday . . . our honor": ibid., pp. 151–52.

          "A train . . . anything": ibid., pp. 155–56, 159.

123   "I saw . . . and blood": ibid., pp. 163–64.

123–24   "We arrived . . . days": ibid., pp. 176–77.

124   "I am . . . about it": ibid., pp. 179–81.

125   "The weather . . . water": ibid., p. 188.

          "For the . . . General": ibid., pp. 189–93.

126   "This morning . . . Commission": ibid., pp. 193–96.

          "I have . . . now": ibid., pp. 202, 205, 207.

Biddy Mason

Abbreviations used are: Brown—*Autobiography of John Brown*, Hayden—*The Power of Place*

Page

132   "All things . . . weather": Brown, p. 88.

          "Last night . . . hurricane": ibid., p. 89.

133   "We were . . . month": ibid., p. 93.

          "June 1 . . . by": ibid., p. 97.

          "August 29 . . . die": ibid., p. 101.

          "September 1 . . . inches": ibid.

135   "has supported . . . family": Hayden, p. 148.

          "I always . . . here": ibid., p. 146.

136   "all . . . fear": ibid., p. 150.

          "She was . . . families": ibid., p. 153.

137   "the sum . . . dollars": ibid., p. 162.

          "Her . . . assistance": Kate Bradley Stovall, "The Negro Woman in Los
             Angeles," *Los Angeles Times*, February 12, 1909.

          "If you . . . receives": Hayden, p. 167.

138   "She . . . her": Gregory Crouch, "Early Black Heroine of L.A. Finally Receives
             Her Due," *Los Angeles Times*, March 28, 1988: 20.

138   "was . . . homestead": Hayden, p. 160.
139   "It took . . . history": Bob Pool, "Proud Legacy," *Los Angeles Times*, July 31,
       1991: B8.

Peggy Hull

Abbreviations used are: O'Donnell—"Peggy Hull"; Kuhn—"Peggy Hull Deuell:
Correspondent on Four Fronts"; PH—Peggy Hull's newspaper articles; PHDC—Peggy
Hull Deuell Collection, Kansas Collection, University of Kansas Libraries, Lawrence,
Kansas; Benjamin—*Eye Witness*; SB—*The Wars of Peggy Hull*, biography of Peggy Hull by
Wilda M. Smith and Eleanor A. Bogart

Page
140   "wouldn't . . . Hull": "The Post Goes Visiting—Peggy Hull Deuell—First
       Woman War Correspondent." *San Clemente* [CA] *Post*, Aug. 6, 1953, PHDC,
       quoted in SB, p. 30.
       "determined . . . somebody": SB, p. 11.
142   "pearl gray . . . hat": *Sunday Times* [Charleston, SC], Oct. 22, 1916, quoted in
       SB, p. 55.
142–43 "I had . . . veteran": ibid.
143   "Water wagons . . . quit": PH, *Marysville Advocate Democrat*, May 1, 1919: 1,
       quoted in SB, p. 57.
145   "When word . . . Pershing": Kuhn, p. 5.
146   "How perfectly . . . voice": "Plucky Yankee Girl Reporter First War
       Correspondent to Win British Censor's Praise," PHDC, quoted in SB,
       p. 71.
       "thick set . . . disapproval": PH, *El Paso Morning Times*, July 18, 1917: 1.
146–47 "What do . . . and ink": ibid.
147–48 "He appeared . . . go home": *Chicago Tribune*, Army Edition (Paris, France),
       Aug. 18, 1917, quoted in SB, p. 88.
148   "Why . . . all right": PH, *El Paso Morning Times*, Aug. 9, 1917.
       "It is . . . from me": PH, "Dear Officers and So; diers [sic] of the A.E.F."
       PHDC, quoted in SB, pp. 112–13.
149   "Your stories . . . you!": O'Donnell, p. 83.
       "No woman . . . Vladivostok": ibid.
149–50 "The Bearer . . . spared": SB, p. 138.
150   "I was . . . accomplish": William S. Graves, *America's Siberian Adventure,
       1919–1920* (New York: Arno Press and the *New York Times*, 1971), 56: quoted
       in SB, p. 155.
       "Of course . . . either": ibid., pp. 147–48.
151   "Go . . . correspondent": Stegman interview, quoted in SB, p. 189.
       "for three . . . misery": PH, *Chicago Tribune*, Jan. 29, 1932.

152   "pretended . . . identification": Byron E. Guise, "Peggy Hull, Remembered Here as an Ambitious Girl, First Accredited Woman War Correspondent, Again Reports the War," *Marshall County News* [Marysville, KS], Feb. 10, 1944, quoted in SB, p. 191.

153   "smoking . . . intervals": PH, "Open Grave in Shanghai." From Benjamin, 8.

153–54 "Not more . . . battlefield": ibid.

154–56 Excerpts from Hull's dispatches originally appeared in the *New York Daily News*, quoted in SB, pp. 195–98.

156–57 "made a . . . feeling": PH to Byron E. Guise, quoted in SB, p. 198.

       "You made . . . forgotten": Wilda M. Smith and Eleanor A. Bogart, "Deuell, Henrietta Eleanor Goodnough," *The Handbook of Texas Online* [http://www.tsha.utexas.edu/handbook/online/articles/print/DD/fdetm.html].

SELECTED BIBLIOGRAPHY

Author's Note

Granger, A. G. "Through the Yangtze Gorges to Wan Hsien." *Natural History* 24, no. 2 (1924): 224–35.

———. "Wintering over a Fire Basket in Szechuan." *Natural History* 24, no. 3 (1924): 366–80.

———. "Rescuing a Little-known Chinese Art: How an Explorer's Wife 'Discovered' a Fascinating Style of Peasant Embroidery in Far Western China, and Helped to Save It from Oblivion." *Natural History* 61, no. 1 (1938): 52–61.

Morgan, Vincent L., and Spencer G. Lucas. *Walter Granger, 1872–1941, Paleontologist.* Albuquerque, NM: New Mexico Museum of Natural History and Science, 2002.

Louise Boyd

Boyd, Louise Arner. *The Fiord Region of East Greenland.* Vols. 1 and 2. New York: American Geographical Society, 1935.

———. *The Coast of Northeast Greenland with Hydrographic Studies in the Greenland Sea.* New York: American Geographical Society, 1948.

———. *Polish Countrysides, Photographs and Narrative by Louise A. Boyd.* New York: American Geographical Society, 1937.

Curtis, Charlotte. "Society Glitters in San Francisco." *New York Times,* September 12, 1963.

———. "Geographical Award Goes to Louise Boyd," December 5, 1939.

———. "Louise Arner Boyd Dies at 84: Led Expeditions to the Arctic," September 17, 1972.

New York Times, "Accepts Honor for Miss Boyd," February 14, 1932.

———. "Aided Amundsen Search," December 9, 1928.

———. "American Girl Shot 11 Bears in Arctic," September 26, 1926.

Olds, Elizabeth Fagg. *Women of the Four Winds: The Adventures of Four of America's First Women Explorers.* Boston: Houghton Mifflin Co., 1985.

Owen, Russell. "A Woman Makes Her Mark in a Man's Domain." *New York Times,* May 1, 1938.

Petersen, Anne. "Women Here Are Preparing for Voyages of Exploration." *New York Times,* February 14, 1937.

———. "Two Warships Begin Hunt for Amundsen," June 28, 1928.

———. "Woman Describes Voyage to Arctic," December 2, 1938.

———. "Woman Explorer Honored by Army," March 19, 1949.

———. "Woman Explorer Sailing for North," May 5, 1937.

Polk, Milbry, and Mary Tiegreen. *Women of Discovery: A Celebration of Intrepid Women Who Explored the World.* London: Scriptum Editions, 2001.

San Rafael Independent, "Arctic Search Fun for Marin 'Tomboy,'" November 21, 1928.

Sherr, Lynn, and Jurate Kazickas. *Susan B. Anthony Slept Here: A Guide to American Women's Landmarks.* New York: Times Books, 1994.

Stefoff, Rebecca. *Women of the World.* Oxford: Oxford University Press, 1992.

Mary Gibson Henry

Buckley, Thomas. "Woman Botanist Still Busy at 79." *New York Times,* May 29, 1963.

Henry, Mary Gibson. "Mary Gibson Henry: An Autobiography." *Plant Life,* 6, no. 1 (1950).

———. "Collecting Plants Beyond the Frontier in Northern British Columbia, 1931 Expedition." Reprinted from *National Horticultural Magazine,* January 1934.

———. "Collecting Plants Beyond the Frontier in Northern British Columbia." Reprinted from *National Horticultural Magazine,* April 1935.

———. "Collecting Plants Beyond the Frontier in Northern British Columbia, Part VII, 1933 Expedition." Reprinted from *National Horticultural Magazine,* April 1949.

———. "Exploring and Plant Collecting in Northern British Columbia." Reprinted from the 1933 yearbook of the Pennsylvania Horticultural Society.

New Yorker, "Lady Botanist," July 27, 1963.

New York Times, "Mrs. Mary Henry, Botanist, Was 82," April 18, 1967.

Royal Botanic Garden Edinburgh. "The Impact of the Plant-hunters." http://www.rbge. org.uk/rbge/web/news/planthunt.jsp.

Whittle, Tyler. *The Plant Hunters: Tales of the Botanist Explorers Who Enriched Our Gardens.* Guilford, CT: Lyons Press, 1997.

Juana Briones

Bowman, J. N. "Juana Briones de Miranda." *The Historical Society of Southern California* 39, no. 3 (1957).

Coleman, Sarah. "Juana Briones: A Feminist Pioneer in North Beach." *Feminista! The Journal of Feminist Construction* 1, no. 7 (1997). http://www.feminista.com/archives/v1n7/ coleman.html.

Fava, Florence. *Los Altos Hills.* Woodside, CA: Gilbert Richards Publications, 1979.

"Foundations of SF Matriarch's Adobe House Unearthed in Dig: Major Discovery at Presidio by Stanford Archaeologists," 11/6/2004. http://www.presidio.gov/TrustManagement/TrustPress/pressrelease/ArchaeologyDiscovery/htm.

Graham, Doug. "Juana Briones Home Threatened." http://www.cyberstars.com/bp-news/dec96/history.html.

Voss, Barbara L. "The Briones Sisters: Guadalupe, Juana, and Maria de la Luz," in *The Archaeology of El Presidio de San Francisco: Culture Contact, Gender, and Ethnicity in a Spanish-colonial Community.* PhD dissertation, University of California, Berkeley, 2002.

Alice Hamilton

Hamilton, Alice. "A Woman of Ninety Looks at Her World." *Atlantic Monthly*, September 1961.

———. *Exploring the Dangerous Trades: The Autobiography of Alice Hamilton, M.D.* Boston: Northeastern University Press, 1985. First published 1943 by Little, Brown and Company.

———. "Nineteen Years in the Poisonous Trades." *Harper's*. October 1929.

———. *Industrial Poisons in the United States.* New York: Macmillan, 1925.

———. *Industrial Toxicology.* New York: Harper, 1934.

———. *Lead Poisoning in the Manufacture of Storage Batteries.* Washington, D.C.: Government Printing Office, 1915.

———. *Lead Poisoning in the Smelting and Refining of Lead.* Washington, D.C.: Government Printing Office, 1914.

———. *Women in the Lead Industries.* Washington, D.C.: Government Printing Office, 1919.

James, Edward T. et al., eds. *Notable American Women: A Biographical Dictionary.* Vol. 2. Cambridge, MA: The Belknap Press, 1971.

Kovarik, Bill. "The Radium Girls," http://www.runet.edu/~wkovarik/hist1/radium.html.

Sicherman, Barbara. *Alice Hamilton: A Life in Letters.* Cambridge, MA: Harvard University Press, 1984.

Woolf, S. J. "Triumphs of a Pioneer Doctor." *New York Times Magazine*, November 9, 1947.

Mary McLeod Bethune

Bethune, Mary McLeod. "I'll Never Turn Back No More!" *Opportunity*, November 1938.

———. "Faith That Moved a Dump Heap." *Who, the Magazine about People*, June 1941.

———. "My Last Will and Testament," *Ebony*, August 1955.

———. Mary McLeod Bethune Papers, The Bethune-Cookman College Collection, 1922–1955. http://www.lexisnexis.com/academic/guides/african_american/bethune/bethune.asp.

Hine, Darlene Clark, and Kathleen Thompson. *A Shining Thread of Hope: The History of Black Women in America.* New York: Broadway Books, 1998.

Hine, Darlene Clark et al., eds. *Black Women in America.* New York: Carlson Publishing, 1993.

James, Edward T. et al., eds. *Notable American Women: A Biographical Dictionary.* Vol. 2. Cambridge, MA: The Belknap Press, 1971.

Kelso, Richard. *Building a Dream: Mary McLeod Bethune's School.* Austin, TX: Raintree Steck-Vaughn, 1993.

McCluskey, Audrey Thomas, and Elaine M. Smith, eds. *Mary McLeod Bethune: Building a Better World.* Bloomington: Indiana University Press, 2002.

Peare, Catherine Owens. *Mary McLeod Bethune.* New York: The Vanguard Press, 1951.

Sicherman, Barbara and Carol Hurd Green, eds. *Notable American Women: The Modern Period.* Cambridge, MA: The Belknap Press, 1980.

Katharine Wormeley

Bacon, Georgeanna and Eliza Woolsey Howland. *Letters of a Family during the War for the Union, 1861–1865.* New Haven, CT: Tuttle, Morehouse & Taylor, 1899.

Brockett, L. P. *Woman's Work in the Civil War: A Record of Heroism, Patriotism and Patience.* Philadelphia: Ziegler, McCurdy & Co., 1867.

Censer, Jane Turner, ed. *The Papers of Frederick Law Olmsted.* Vol. 4: *Defending the Union: The Civil War and the U.S. Sanitary Commission, 1861–1863.* Baltimore, MD: The Johns Hopkins University Press, 1986.

Garrison, Nancy Scripture. *With Courage and Delicacy: Civil War on the Peninsula: Women and the U.S. Sanitary Commission.* Mason City, IA: Savas Publishing Co, 1999.

Giesberg, Judith Ann. *Civil War Sisterhood: The U.S. Sanitary Commission and Women's Politics in Transition.* Boston: Northeastern University Press, 2000.

James, Edward T. et al., eds. *Notable American Women: A Biographical Dictionary.* Vol. 3. Cambridge, MA: The Belknap Press, 1971.

Wormeley, Katharine Prescott. *The Other Side of War, with the Army of the Potomac: Letters from the Headquarters of the United States Sanitary Commission during the Peninsular Campaign in Virginia in 1862.* Boston: Ticknor and Co., 1889.

Biddy Mason

Brown, John. *Autobiography of John Brown.* Salt Lake City, UT: Stevens & Wallis, Inc., 1941.

Bunch, Lonnie G. *Black Angelenos: The Afro-American in Los Angeles, 1850–1950.* Los Angeles: Afro-American Museum, 1988.

Crouch, Gregory. "Early Black Heroine of L.A. Finally Receives Her Due." *Los Angeles Times,* March 28, 1988.

Hayden, Dolores. *The Power of Place: Urban Landscapes as Public History.* Cambridge, MA: The MIT Press, 1995.

Mungen, Donna. *The Life and Times of Biddy Mason.* N.p., 1978.

Oliver, Myrna. "A Lot of History." *Los Angeles Times,* November 17, 1989.

Pool, Bob. "Proud Legacy." *Los Angeles Times,* July 31, 1991.

Stovall, Kate Bradley. "The Negro Woman in Los Angeles." *Los Angeles Times,* February 12, 1909.

Whiteson, Leon. "The Landscape as Parable." *Los Angeles Times,* February 19, 1990.

Peggy Hull

Benjamin, Robert Spiers, ed. *Eye Witness.* New York: Alliance Book Corp., 1940.

Hull, Peggy.
   Chicago Tribune, January 29, 1932.
   Cleveland Plain Dealer, September 21, 1916.
   ———. August 4, 1944.
   ———. September 27, 1945.
   El Paso Morning Times, July 18, 1917.
   ———. August 9, 1917.

Kuhn, Irene Corbally. "Peggy Hull Deuell: Correspondent on Four Fronts." *Overseas Press Club Bulletin*, July 15, 1967.

O'Donnell, Jack. "Peggy Hull," *The Ladies Home Journal*, April 1920.

Smith, Wilda M., and Eleanor A. Bogart. *The Wars of Peggy Hull: The Life and Times of a War Correspondent*. El Paso, TX: Texas Western Press, 1991.

———. "Deuell, Henrietta Eleanor Goodnough." *The Handbook of Texas Online* [http://www.tsha.utexas.edu/handbook/online/articles/print/DD/fdetm.html].

WEBLIOGRAPHY

Author's Note (Walter and Anna Granger)

Morgan, Vin. The Granger Papers Project [http://users.rcn.com/granger.nh.ultranet].

Louise Boyd

Female Explorers. "Louise Arner Boyd: Arctic Explorer" [http://www.femexplorers.com/article1008.html].

Mary Gibson Henry

"The Impact of the Plant-hunters" [http://www.rbge.org.uk/rbge/web/news/planthunt.jsp].

Kaplan, Kim. United States Department of Agriculture. "The Plant Hunters" [http://www.ars.usda.gov/is/kids/plants/story4/hunters.htm].

Juana Briones

Juana Briones Heritage Foundation. "Who's Juana?" [http://www.brioneshouse.org/juana.html].

Voss, Barbara. Stanford University Research at the Presidio of San Francisco. Tennessee Hollow Watershed Archaeological Project. Presidio Web [http://www.stanford.edu/group/presidio/juana.html].

Alice Hamilton

The Chemical Heritage Foundation. "Alice Hamilton" Chemical Achievers [http://chemheritage.org/EducationalServices/Chemach/hnec/ah.html].

Mary McLeod Bethune

National Park Service. Mary McLeod Bethune Council House. "Meet Mrs. Bethune" [http://www.nps.gov/mamc/bethune/meet/frame.htm].

Katherine Wormeley

Shotgun's Home of the American Civil War. "Sanitary Commission to the Rescue" [http://www.civilwarhome.com/sanitarycommtorescue.htm].

Biddy Mason

University of Southern California. "Biddy Mason's Place: A Passage of Time" [http://www.usc.edu/isd/archives/la/pubart/Downtown/Broadway/Biddy_Mason].

Peggy Hull

The General Libraries of Texas at Austin. "The Handbook of Texas Online" [http://www.tsha.utexas.edu/handbook/online/articles/DD/fdetm.html].

PHOTO CREDITS

Photo Credits

Katharine Wormeley

103 MOLLUS Collection (Mass. Commandery), Photographic Archives, U.S. Army Military History Institute, Carlisle Barracks, PA.

106 From *The Papers of Frederick Law Olmsted*. Vol. 4, *Defending the Union, the Civil War, and the U.S. Sanitary Commission, 1861–1863*. Edited by Jane Turner Censer (1986) by permission of the Johns Hopkins University Press.

109 From *The Papers of Frederick Law Olmsted*, Vol. 4, *Defending the Union, the Civil War, and the U.S. Sanitary Commission, 1861–1863*. Edited by Jane Turner Censer (1986) by permission of the Johns Hopkins University Press.

Biddy Mason

128 Penny Colman.

131 Penny Colman.

139 Dolores Hayden.

Peggy Hull

141 Peggy Hull Deuell Collection, Kansas Collection, University of Kansas Libraries.

144 *El Paso Morning Times.*

147 Peggy Hull Deuell Collection, Kansas Collection, University of Kansas Libraries.

152 Peggy Hull Deuell Collection, Kansas Collection, University of Kansas Libraries.

INDEX

(Page numbers in **boldface** refer to illustrations.)

9 780805 097375